P9-BBU-782

The Los Angeles Times Book of
Christmas Entertaining
Creative Ways to Celebrate the Holidays

The Los Angeles Times Book of
Christmas Entertaining
Creative Ways to Celebrate the Holidays

The Los Angeles Times Book of
Christmas Entertaining
Creative Ways to Celebrate the Holidays

by Dawn Navarro

Recipes Compiled and Edited by Betsy Balsley

Harry N. Abrams, Inc., Publishers, New York

Project Manager: Lois Brown
Editor: Ruth Peltason
Designer: Melissa Feldman

Library of Congress Cataloging in Publication Data

Navarro, Dawn.
The Los Angeles times book of Christmas entertaining.
1. Christmas cookery.   2. Christmas decorations.
3. Entertaining.   4. Handicraft.   I. Balsley, Betsy.
II. Los Angeles times.   III. Title.
TX739.N33   1985   793.2'2   85 – 4061
ISBN 0–8109–1290–2

Illustrations copyright © 1985 by *Los Angeles Times*

Published in 1985 by Harry N. Abrams, Incorporated,
New York. All rights reserved. No part of the contents of
this book may be reproduced without the written
permission of the publishers

Printed and bound in Japan

Contents

Introduction

Whether you choose to entertain a small gathering of friends or plan an elaborate gala, the Christmas season is a time to show off your talents.

We've planned this book with just that in mind. Each chapter is a combination of crafts projects and recipes for traditional buffets, light suppers for late evening entertaining after the tree is trimmed, desserts, and children's parties. For instance, your kitchen can be used as a workshop in the "Bake and Give" chapter for baking bread and cookies to be wrapped in colorful cellophane, blending spices to be packed in acetate boxes, and making your own bottled herbed oil. All of these edible gifts can then be arranged in beautiful baskets trimmed with Christmas ribbons.

Children will love being the star attractions at our Christmas portrait party as they sit on Santa's lap and pose for the camera. And the adults will love the Standing Rib Roast, accompanied by the Yorkshire Pudding, waiting to be eaten on a seasonally decorated buffet table. In the "Holiday Workshop" chapter, children will enjoy making their own garlands, winter wreaths, window ornaments, and clay necklaces. We've even brought back the quilting party and provided all the instructions for gathering materials and choosing fabrics.

All of the crafts can be accomplished with little effort. In putting them together we kept in mind that each project must be "do-able." The materials may be acquired easily without great expense, and arranged ahead of time. To make the crafts pictured in each of the chapters, refer to the back of the book where we provide you with all of the instructions, diagrams, and how-to illustrations that you'll need.

The recipes are traditional in nature and will satisfy your creative cooking desires. They are neither time-consuming nor will their cost conflict with your gift budget. Most can be made ahead of time or, as with our omelets (with a variety of fillings), prepared at the party itself. But we can't guarantee you won't want to do your own pairing of recipes with crafts projects. We also can't guarantee that once you've looked at the book, you won't create some projects on your own.

Christmas is a time for family and friends to come together in the spirit of the season. There is no better way to accomplish this than to gather those close to you, entertain them by giving them a way to be creative, and serve them food that they'll greatly enjoy.

A Cat Quilt

As each holiday season draws near all of our best efforts are directed toward planning a celebration full of memories. Whether for a Christmas bazaar or as a personal endeavor, making a quilt can start the Christmas festivities. Family and friends can work together as quilters on this handmade treasure. If you find you don't quite have enough time to put together your quilting party, we've also included ideas for making a cat pillow, teddy bears, country dolls, and wood-turning toys. So no matter what you make, you'll have plenty of good reasons to arrange for a gathering of friends.

Quilts are made either by piecing or appliquéing. A pieced quilt has a top layer of material composed of hundreds of small swatches of fabric stitched together. The appliqué quilt's top layer is one solid layer of fabric with free-floating forms of material stitched down to the surface. Both types of quilts are finished in the same manner—the top is layered on a filler of combed cotton or polyester batting and then placed on the bottom fabric. The quilt is basted together to hold all three layers of fabrics and filler in place ready to be quilted—either machine quilted or stretched on a wooden frame for hand quilting.

Quilt patterns have endless possibilities for creativity with choices of fabric, color, and sizing. Almost all pieced quilts are geometric, with abstract arrangements of circles, triangles, rectangles, and squares. The "cat concept" pictured here incorporates the techniques of classic pieced quilts into a new contemporary pattern and features all the techniques of pieced work—appliqué, embroidery, and quilting.

Planning Your Quilting Party

The first step toward planning a quilting party is gathering materials. Color is the first impression when you look at a quilt, so look for the perfect fabric in a store or use favorite remnants that you've been gathering over the years. Look for colors that are balanced and complementary in shades. The colors must form their own design scheme within the pattern. Here, the selection of dark-colored fabric and a light-colored striped fabric enhanced the reverse-image design of the cat quilt. The background and trim colors were carefully selected to contrast and blend with the cat's colors.

Quilts are meant to be passed on as heirlooms, so when you purchase materials consider how the fabric will hold up. When the quilt is washed, will it become limp or warped or lumpy? Will the colors quickly fade? Is the thread strong? Can the material withstand a lot of use without showing age? Test your choices of color and fabric by washing a sample of the fabric.

Have all your materials together before the project begins. Your quilters can then easily see and understand your ideas when everything is ready.

You should precut all the pieces for the quilt to assure that all sizes are consistent. Several people can help with sewing; all you need to do is mark on your sewing machine with tape the exact seam allowance needed for all piecing. (The design of the cat quilt, based on straight lines, was stitched on a machine.) Have your quilters help do such tasks as count and organize the pieces for sewing into blocks, cut threads, iron pieces, embroider the cat faces, sew and stuff the cat toys, and appliqué the toys. Plan the work for each quilter.

So many parts of the quilting project are appropriate for a party—piecing the top layer of the quilt, embroidering the blocks for the cat's face, hand quilting or appliquéing the cat toys to finish the quilt—as are the other ideas that follow.

12

Wood-Turning Toys

Spindles, newels, balusters, and wood turnings are just some of the bits and pieces used to make these wood-turning toys. Although ordinarily used as embellishments on buildings and furniture, with a little imagination they can spring to life as horses, clown heads (ours is a variation of a jack-in-the-box), or a star-topped tower.

These toys are terrific for Christmas decorating and are easy to make. Nails and glue aren't needed and there's very little cutting. The toys are held together with dowels and can be taken apart and put back together again; painting is easy too. A drill to make holes for the dowel joints and a hand-saw for the platforms are the only tools needed.

Expect these toys to be oversized—the star-topped tower is almost three feet tall. Be prepared to work on a large scale and look for wood turnings that have unusual shapes. The toys portrayed here can be used as a guide. Have fun finding your own selection of wood turnings, and creating your own special toys.

Country Dolls

They arrive on Christmas morning wrapped in rainbow tissue, wearing their prettiest dresses. Their braids and dainty curls are tied with crisp new ribbons and their faces carry an expression of wide-eyed surprise. No two country dolls are ever alike because the personal touches of the dollmaker give each one its own enchanting style.

Search through drawers and children's toy boxes for material. Comb hair into different arrangements and tie with a satin bow. And finally, paint a face that captures an exquisite simple mood.

The cat quilt and matching pillow look cozy in this sunny bedroom

Gathering colorful fabrics and charming accessories are part of the fun in creating handmade dolls

14

OPPOSITE *These teddy bears are easy to make, and varied by the choice of fabric*

Teddy Bears

It is hard to imagine Christmas without a teddy bear. It should be a warm companion, a good listener, and soft and huggable.

The outstanding character of a teddy bear should be determined by its shape. The fabric, color, and detail stitching create a unique bear. The multi-colored textured wool used on our teddy bear delivers a personality quite the opposite of a teddy bear made with quilted floral cotton. A shiny, hot-colored, plastic-coated linen gives flash to a bear . . . pastel silk, an aura of gentility. Accessories such as a cowboy hat, a pin-striped vest, or a ballerina costume all add character.

Easy to make, teddy bears lend themselves to a group effort. As many as ten bears can be hand-crafted at a party if all helpers are organized. A twelve-inch sitting bear is the most accommodating, but when working with different sizes and materials experiment to see how the various fabrics work when firmly stuffed with polyester filling. If possible, have one bear completed for a model. Please make sure that buttons are sewn on tightly so that children—particularly young children —aren't able to pull them off. Of course, if you do have young children, you could leave off the button eyes altogether.

Coffee and Coffee Cakes

The conviviality of a cup of coffee, accompanied by an enticing choice of time-tested coffee cakes, adds the perfect touch of warmth and welcome to a Christmas quilting party. What better way to show appreciation for your quilters' time and efforts than to offer them a delicious, steaming cup of a spicy cinnamon-flavored coffee, or perhaps one spiked with a hint of Irish whiskey. A fruit-filled coffee cake will add a festive touch to coffee break time during the activities and send the crew back to work with renewed energy.

If the quilting project is a club activity, let the group's best bakers bring the coffee cakes; but if it's a friendly get-together, you can bake a batch of coffee cakes in advance and freeze them. In either case, the flavored coffees will be last-minute projects. But all are easy and very quick to prepare. See pages 20–25 for the recipes.

With little effort, wood turnings are easily assembled, as in the hobbyhorse and jack-in-the-box shown above

18

This painted star-topped tower is almost three feet tall

19

Coconut Coffee Ring

¼ cup brown sugar, packed
¼ cup chopped filberts or other nuts
¾ cup flake coconut
2 cups sifted flour
⅓ cup granulated sugar
2 ½ teaspoons baking powder
1 teaspoon salt
⅓ cup shortening
1 egg, lightly beaten
⅓ cup milk
3 tablespoons butter or margarine, melted
Glaze

Combine brown sugar, filberts, and ½ cup coconut, and set aside. Sift flour with granulated sugar, baking powder, and salt. Cut in shortening until mixture is crumbly. Combine egg and milk, add to flour mixture, and stir until a soft dough is formed.

Turn dough out onto a lightly floured board and knead for 30 seconds. Roll into an 18 × 9-inch rectangle. Brush with part of the melted butter, then spread with coconut-filbert mixture. Roll jelly roll fashion starting from long side. Wet edge to seal. Bring ends together and seal to form a ring.

Place ring on an ungreased baking sheet. Slice through, almost to center, in 1-inch intervals. Turn each slice so cut side is exposed. Brush with remaining butter. Bake at 400 degrees for 20 to 25 minutes. Place coffee ring on cake rack and drizzle with Glaze while ring is still hot. Sprinkle with remaining ¼ cup coconut.

Makes about 12 to 14 servings.

Glaze
1 cup sifted powdered sugar
1 tablespoon hot milk, approximately

To make glaze, combine powdered sugar and hot milk.

Holiday Star

2 cups flour
1 tablespoon baking powder
1 teaspoon salt
¾ teaspoon ground ginger
¼ cup shortening
½ to ¾ cup milk
Fig Filling
Orange Glaze

Sift together flour, baking powder, salt, and ginger. Cut in shortening until mixture resembles coarse crumbs. Blend in enough milk to make a soft dough. Turn onto lightly floured surface and knead gently for 30 seconds. Cut in half, then roll each half into a 9-inch circle. Place 1 circle on ungreased baking sheet or in a 9-inch shallow round cake pan. Spread pastry with Fig Filling, leaving a ½-inch margin around outside edge. Top with second circle. Press edges together to seal. Slash top circle of dough to form a star, cutting from center of circle to within 1 inch of edge. Lift each point and twist over once sideways. Bake at 450 degrees for 12 to 15 minutes. Brush top immediately with Orange Glaze when done. Serve warm.

Makes 6 to 8 servings.

Fig Filling
1 (8-ounce) package dried figs, chopped
½ cup chopped pecans
¾ cup orange juice
2 tablespoons butter or margarine
1 teaspoon grated orange peel
½ teaspoon ground ginger

In a small saucepan, combine figs, pecans, juice, butter, orange peel, and ginger. Simmer for 5 minutes, stirring frequently.

Orange Glaze
2 to 3 teaspoons orange juice
½ cup powdered sugar

Stir juice into sugar, a teaspoon at a time, until a smooth consistency is reached.

Cranberry Kuchen

2 cups sifted flour
1 tablespoon baking powder
¾ teaspoon salt
½ cup sugar
5 tablespoons butter or margarine
1 egg, beaten
½ cup milk
2½ cups cranberries, coarsely chopped
Topping

Sift flour, baking powder, salt, and sugar together. Cut in butter with pastry blender until crumbly. Mix beaten egg and milk, and add to flour mixture. Stir slowly to mix, then beat until well blended. Spread batter evenly in 8-inch square buttered baking dish. Sprinkle chopped cranberries evenly over top. Sprinkle Topping over cranberries. Bake at 375 degrees for 30 to 35 minutes. Serve warm.

Makes 9 squares.

Topping
¼ cup flour
½ cup sugar
½ teaspoon ground cloves
3 tablespoons butter or margarine

Mix flour, sugar, and cloves together. Cut in butter until mixture is crumbly.

Pear-Topped Ring Cake

3 small or 2 medium pears
2 tablespoons butter or margarine
1 teaspoon grated orange peel
1 cup sugar
¼ cup shortening
1 egg
1 teaspoon vanilla
½ cup milk
¼ cup orange juice
2 cups sifted flour

1 tablespoon baking powder
1 teaspoon salt

Peel, halve, and core pears. Cut each half lengthwise into 4 or 5 slices. Melt butter in a 6½- or 7-cup ring mold, swirling to coat inside. Mix orange peel with ¼ cup of the sugar and spoon into bottom of mold. Arrange pear slices over sugar. Blend remaining ¾ cup sugar with shortening, egg, and vanilla. Blend in milk and orange juice. Sift flour with baking powder and salt and add to creamed mixture, beating until smooth. Spoon batter over pears. Bake at 375 degrees for 35 minutes or until top is golden, and toothpick inserted in center comes out clean. Cool in pan for 5 to 10 minutes, then invert onto serving plate.

Makes 8 servings.

Fruit Roll

1 egg
3 cups buttermilk biscuit mix
Milk
Apricot or *Prune Filling* (page 24)
½ cup powdered sugar

Beat egg and add biscuit mix and ¾ cup milk. Stir to form a soft dough. Turn out onto a lightly floured surface and knead just until smooth. Pat or roll out to a 10 × 8-inch rectangle. Spread with Apricot or Prune Filling. Roll up jelly roll fashion starting at wide side. Seal seam by pinching firmly to roll. Place sealed side down on ungreased baking sheet. Cut almost through roll with scissors at 1-inch intervals, then carefully curve roll, opening up the cuts slightly. Bake at 400 degrees for 20 minutes. While warm, drizzle with glaze made by mixing powdered sugar with 2 to 3 teaspoons milk.

Makes 8 to 10 servings.

OVERLEAF *Top shelf, left to right: Fruit Swirl Coffee Cake; Pear-Topped Ring Cake; bottom, left to right: Coconut Coffee Ring; crescent-shaped Fruit Roll; Holiday Star; Cranberry Kuchen; Cheese-Filled Coffee Cake*

Apricot or *Prune Filling*
½ pound dried pitted apricots or prunes
Water
½ teaspoon allspice
Sugar
Grated peel of 1 lemon
1 tablespoon lemon juice

Place fruit in a small saucepan with enough water to cover. Bring to a boil, reduce heat, and simmer until fruit is tender, about 30 minutes. Drain fruit and chop fine. Stir in allspice, sugar to taste, lemon peel, and juice. Cool.

Fruit Swirl Coffee Cake

2 cups sifted flour
1 cup sugar
½ teaspoon cinnamon
½ teaspoon nutmeg
¾ cup (1 ½ sticks) butter or margarine
2 teaspoons baking powder
1 teaspoon salt
2 eggs, beaten
½ cup buttermilk
½ cup thick preserves or marmalade

Combine ½ cup of the flour, ½ cup of the sugar, cinnamon, and nutmeg. Cut in ¼ cup of the butter with a pastry blender until mixture resembles fine crumbs. Set aside.

Combine remaining 1½ cups flour and ½ cup sugar with the baking powder and salt. Cut in remaining ½ cup butter with pastry blender until mixture resembles fine crumbs. Add eggs and buttermilk. Stir just until dry ingredients are moistened. Spread batter in greased 9 × 5-inch loaf pan. Spoon preserves over batter and cut through mixture with knife to swirl preserves into batter. Sprinkle reserved crumb mixture over top. Bake at 350 degrees for 35 to 40 minutes or until cake shrinks slightly from sides of pan.

Makes 8 to 10 servings.

Cheese-Filled Coffee Cakes

7 cups sifted flour
Sugar
1 teaspoon salt
⅛ teaspoon cardamom
2 packages dry yeast
1 cup milk
¾ cup butter or margarine
3 whole eggs
Cheese Filling
1 egg white
1 tablespoon water

In a large bowl, thoroughly mix 2 cups of the flour, ¾ cup sugar, salt, cardamom, and yeast. Combine milk and butter in a saucepan and heat only until liquid is warm. Butter does not need to melt. Gradually add this to the dry ingredients, and beat for 2 minutes at medium speed with electric mixer, scraping bowl occasionally. Add whole eggs and ½ cup of flour, or enough to make a thick batter. Beat at high speed for 2 minutes, scraping bowl occasionally.

Stir in enough more flour to make a soft, moist dough. Divide dough into halves. Roll each half to a 12 × 8-inch rectangle. Spread filling lengthwise down the center of each rectangle. Make 2-inch diagonal slashes along the sides of the rectangle *not* covered with filling. Fold dough over filling at each end, making what looks like a 1-inch hem. Fold side strips of dough over filling, making it look like a braid. Carefully place rectangles on a greased baking sheet and let rise in warm place until doubled, about 30 minutes. Bake at 375 degrees for 30 minutes. Remove from oven and brush with mixture of lightly beaten egg white and water. Sprinkle with granulated sugar and return to oven for 10 to 15 minutes. Cool on rack.

Makes 2 large coffee cakes.

Cheese Filling
1½ cups creamed cottage cheese
2 egg yolks
¼ teaspoon salt

24

½ teaspoon grated lemon peel
¼ cup sugar

Combine cottage cheese, egg yolks, salt, lemon peel, and sugar. Mix well.

Spicy Joe

6 cups brewed coffee
Cinnamon sticks
12 whole cloves
12 allspice berries
4 cups hot milk
Sugar

As soon as coffee is brewed, add 4 2-inch-long cinnamon sticks, cloves, and allspice. Hold at serving temperature for 15 minutes. Do not allow to boil. Strain into a pitcher. Add milk and mix well. Sweeten to taste with sugar and beat with rotary beater until creamy and foamy. Pour into pretty cups or stemmed glasses, and garnish each with a long cinnamon stick.

Makes 10 to 12 servings.

Café Aruba

8 cups water
1 cup ground coffee
2 tablespoons sugar
Orange peel cut into thin strips
1 orange, peeled and sliced
2 teaspoons bitters
1 cup whipping cream

Fill coffeepot with water. Place ground coffee, 1 tablespoon of the sugar, and ¼ cup orange peel strips in basket. Perk coffee as usual. When done, remove basket and add orange slices and bitters to perked coffee. Cover, and let stand 10 minutes before serving. Whip cream with remaining 1 tablespoon sugar. Serve coffee in footed glasses or tall mugs, topped with a dollop of whipped cream. Garnish with additional strips of orange peel.

Makes 8 servings.

Iced Irish Coffee

3 tablespoons superfine sugar
2 cups hot strong coffee
1 ice tray *Coffee Ice Cubes*
½ cup Irish whiskey
Softly whipped cream
Chocolate coffee beans

Add sugar to hot coffee and stir to dissolve. Chill. Crush enough Coffee Ice Cubes to fill 4 wineglasses. Pour 2 tablespoons Irish whiskey over ice in each glass. Fill glasses almost to top with chilled sweetened coffee. Top with whipped cream and sprinkle with 3 or 4 chocolate coffee beans.

Makes 4 servings.

Coffee Ice Cubes
To make coffee ice cubes, pour double-strength coffee into ice tray and freeze.

Late Evening Get-Together

The days before Christmas are so filled with holiday activities that it is easy to overlook dinner or miss an opportunity to spend time with friends. A late evening party is a perfect solution for sharing the spirit of the holidays after a hectic day of shopping or an evening of caroling. Here we've combined our idea of a luscious wild rice soup with serving containers you can make yourself, as well as a tablecloth of your own design.

Sherried Wild Rice Soup, served with a collection of pine needle basketry, or arranged on a hand-painted tablecloth, is an unexpected pleasure. This warm and aromatic soup is light but filling, and can be prepared early in the day. Accompany it with breadsticks and serve an assortment of Christmas cookies or nuts for dessert.

Pine Needle Basketry

Pine needle basketry is a fitting example of the diversity of handmade crafts. Tightly woven with intricate stitching or enhanced with pine cones, holly, or dried flowers, the results of basket-making are always charming. Pine needle baskets alone or filled with sachets make wonderful gifts and decorative objects. The creative possibilities are almost endless once you've mastered the basic "coiling" technique, which only takes a few minutes.

Our baskets are made with Torrey pine needles and raffia. The Torrey pine tree is native to the coastal areas of Southern California and gathering the needles can be a great winter outing in itself. Other pine needles can be used, but look for needles that are long—up to ten inches is best. While gathering needles also look for pods, dried flowers, and holly or other materials that can be sewn into baskets.

Fabric Art Tablecloth and Scarf

Painting on fabric brings a spectrum of color to winter decorating. It's hard to resist the splashes of blues and greens that make our fabric tablecloth so bright. But we retained the important winter colors —browns, beiges, ambers, yellows, and bright reds—to make our table setting much like a visit to a fall or winter forest environment. Accented with pottery that repeats the color and theme, and with mushrooms, moss, and lettuce, the centerpiece completes an outdoors theme.

To achieve our painted tablecloth we used a French fabric dye-and-resist technique. The line design is drawn on cotton fabric with a natural latex called gutta-percha. The gutta line acts as a "resist" by blocking the dyes from bleeding or blending into one another. We used clear gutta, resulting in a white line, but gutta also is available in various colors, including black, gold, and silver. After the gutta has dried, the dyes are then brushed onto the fabric. These materials are sold in many large art stores, and a few large fabric stores are now beginning to carry the materials as importers make them more readily available.

Sherried Wild Rice Soup

⅔ cup wild rice
2 cups salted water
2 medium leeks, including some green, diced
2 large mushrooms, diced
½ cup butter or margarine
1 cup flour
8 cups hot chicken broth
Salt, pepper
1 cup half and half
3 tablespoons dry sherry

Wash wild rice thoroughly. Place in a heavy saucepan with salted water. Bring to a boil, stir and simmer, covered, for about 45 minutes, until tender but not mushy. Uncover and fluff with a fork. Simmer for an additional 5 minutes. Drain off excess liquid.

Sauté leeks and mushrooms in butter for about 3 minutes, or until soft. Sprinkle vegetables with flour, stirring and cooking until flour is cooked but not browned. Slowly add chicken broth, stirring to blend in flour mixture well. Add rice, and season to taste with salt and pepper. Heat through. Stir in half and half and sherry. Heat gently, but do not boil.

Makes about 12 servings.

If the tablecloth seems like more work than you can handle at this time of year, then try the technique on a small project. Hand-painted silk scarves are inexpensive and wonderful gifts, and only take an hour to make after materials are gathered and you are ready to paint.

The success of this soup depends upon using good, fresh ingredients

Various shapes of pine needle baskets

Handpainted silk scarf

OPPOSITE *The colors in the painted tablecloth are picked up by the green pottery and brightly flecked vegetable soup*

Combining pine needle tableware with plain pottery is an appealing decorating idea

Basket makings: Torrey pine needles and raffia

Wild rice and leeks are a tasty combination

3 The Personal Touch at Christmas

Many of the personal tasks of Christmas, such as addressing cards or invitations, or making small gifts and wrapping them, can be done with a small group of friends. We've offered lots of suggestions for creating your own cards—even making rubber stamps for decoration—and designing gift wrap, which is a much more personal way to package a gift. All of these preparations can be accomplished quite early if you schedule your time; plus, it's easy to bake a variety of dainty quiches as the focal point of your menu for an informal gathering. Tiny quiches are marvelous choices for this type of party as it really doesn't matter if they're hot or just warm when eaten. If time is a problem, make them ahead and rewarm them at the last minute for convenience. Mulled wine or a glass of cool punch and some wonderful chilled pears or other fresh fruits will round out this simple holiday supper. Make a pretty, hand-decorated copy of the recipe, and place it near each of the different quiches; this will make it easier for guests to decide which one they prefer. If there's time, you might even consider making extra copies of your recipes for those who would like to duplicate these tasty savories at home later.

With the menu solved, decorate your work area with the materials needed. A table set with an array of different colored pens and Christmas cards waiting to be addressed is hard to ignore. Or, cover a table with the materials for making rubber stamps as well as lots of solid-colored wrapping papers and ribbons. Ask your guests to bring some materials also—the more you involve your friends, and the more the variety of materials, the better the party.

The Art of the Brush

The Chinese are the undisputed masters of the art of brush painting. It's important to learn the degree of pressure to place on the brush, the angle at which it is held, and the manner of applying the ink or paint. Let the brush create its own movement and rhythm as it reveals the personality of your art. Choosing a brush is important: A soft, round sable brush is perfect for the strokes used to create a rose petal, while a stiff, flat bristle is better for hard-edge graphics.

The personal touch of Christmas can be as simple as a brushstroke made on a card or as decorative gift wrap. It only takes a moment to glide the brush across the paper, even though the enchanting effect of gift wrap or a hand-painted card can leave a lasting impression of your style.

Hand-embellished holiday papers, cards, gift tags, boxes of notes, labels for homemade jams, and baked goods are wonderful ways to show off your creativity. It only takes a few hours of practice to become an accomplished amateur.

Calligraphy

Calligraphy is one of the most graceful ways to send a message. Moreover, the time invested in hand-lettered seasonal greetings, invitations, and labels represents a most personal gift.

Often referred to as writing with a *dancing pen*, calligraphy appears effortless. The ease and fluidity of the pen belie the rigorous hours of training required of the accomplished artisan. An additional plus is that studying calligraphy can be a guide for improving your own handwriting.

Calligraphy can make a fine formal presentation or a casual personal touch on a gift, depending on your individual style and how advanced a calligrapher you become.

Rubber Stamps

Rubber stamps are a simple and fun way to add color and character to your holiday gifts. They're a lot of fun to use; once you build up a collection, you'll discover that stamps are an all-season creative device.

Part of the satisfaction of stamping is the feeling of instant success it gives. Patterns can be made in various ways—one motif may be repeated, or you can alternate images to make your own "story" or image. Stamp out paper place mats for a luncheon or a card game. Or, create name tags for parties, hostess gifts, or lunch bags for the kids. In fact, anything that needs an identity mark is eligible for stamping.

Snowflake Stickers

Quick and easy, stickers can be made in a variety of sizes, and from any adhesive material. They're a simple way to add a personal touch to holiday decorations.

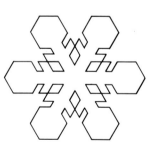

The wide world of pens: Multiline dip and fountain pens, brass-tipped, chisel point, felt, and brush pens gracefully produce lines from as fine as a hairline to 1½ inches wide

A small flat brush is suitable for making a checkerboard pattern

Calligraphy on ribbon and paper is a unique treatment for gift wrap

A good project for a teenager is to enhance a personal diary and notes with brush art and calligraphy

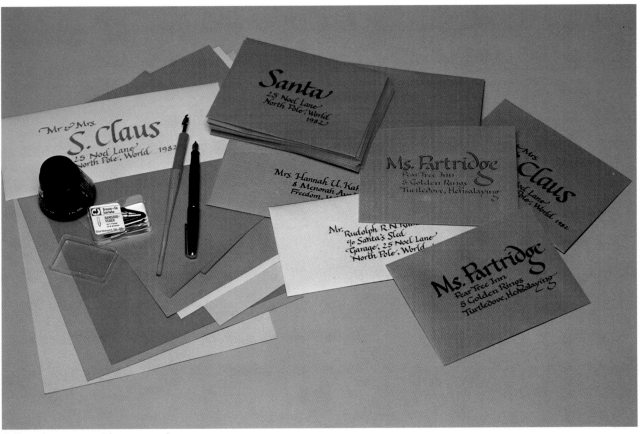

Calligraphy is a graceful way to send a message

39

A sampling of brush strokes . . .

御障子紙
安兵商店特撰

. . . and brushes

41

Use rubber stamps for a quick, simple way to create your own cards and notes

A more unusual treatment is to decorate ribbon using rubber stamps

Stickers are cut from diffraction grating materials

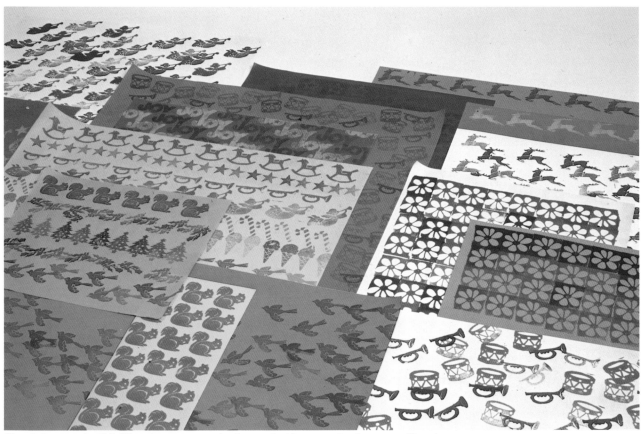

The choices are plentiful: Wrapping papers can be decorated with stamps, brush art, or calligraphy

Large, steel-engraved rubber stamps create a bold, graphic look

A whimsical collection of plastic eraser stamps

44

These cotton overalls were decorated using fabric paints

A gift box with hand-cut stickers

45

Quiche Provençale

Turkey-Almond Quiche tartlets

46

For a no-fuss meal, quiche and fresh fruit are just the ticket

47

Time Out for Quiche

Turkey-Almond Quiche

1 (8-ounce) package cream cheese, softened
1¼ cups milk
2 eggs
½ cup finely chopped toasted almonds
1½ cups chopped cooked turkey
¼ cup finely chopped green onion
1 chicken bouillon cube, crumbled
½ teaspoon salt
¼ teaspoon dry mustard
¼ teaspoon dried basil leaves, crumbled
Pastry for 9- or 10-inch pie shell
Toasted sliced almonds for garnish (optional)
Chopped green onion for garnish (optional)

Beat cream cheese until smooth. Gradually beat in milk. Add eggs one at a time, beating well after each addition. Set aside 1 tablespoon almonds. Stir remaining almonds, turkey, onion, bouillon cube, salt, mustard, and basil into cheese mixture. Roll out pastry and fit into deep 9-inch pie plate, 10-inch tart pan, or eight 4-inch tart pans. Pour filling into pastry shell or shells, sprinkle reserved almonds over top, and bake at 375 degrees for about 50 minutes, or until knife inserted near center comes out clean. Garnish with toasted sliced almonds and chopped green onion, if desired.

Makes 6 to 8 servings.

Quiche Provençale

1 medium onion, sliced
½ cup chopped green pepper
½ teaspoon minced garlic
1 tablespoon oil
2 medium tomatoes, cut in wedges
1 cup sliced zucchini
1 tablespoon minced fresh parsley
1 tablespoon minced fresh basil leaves
¼ teaspoon pepper
1 10-inch pastry shell, unbaked
6 eggs, beaten
1¼ cups half and half

Sauté onion, green pepper, and the garlic in the oil in a large skillet over medium heat until onion is transparent, about 5 minutes. Add the tomatoes, zucchini, parsley, basil, and pepper. Cook, uncovered, 10 minutes, stirring frequently. Drain well.

Brush inside of pastry shell with a small amount of beaten egg. Pierce bottom and sides of shell all over with fork. Bake shell at 450 degrees for 5 minutes, or until light golden brown. Set aside. Reduce oven temperature to 350 degrees. Combine eggs and half and half and pour into pastry shell. Spoon drained vegetables evenly over egg mixture in shell. Bake at 350 degrees for 30 to 35 minutes, or until knife inserted near center comes out clean. Let stand 5 minutes before serving.

Makes 6 to 8 servings.

Dried Beef and Mushroom Quiche

1 (2½-ounce) jar sliced dried beef, chopped
1 cup sliced mushrooms
½ cup chopped onion
2 tablespoons butter or margarine
1 10-inch pastry shell, unbaked
1½ cups shredded Swiss cheese
2 tablespoons flour
4 eggs, lightly beaten
1½ cups milk
Dash cayenne pepper

Sauté dried beef, mushrooms, and onion in butter until onion is tender. Spread mixture evenly over bottom of pastry shell. Toss cheese with flour. Sprinkle over beef mixture. Combine eggs, milk, and cayenne pepper, and pour over mixture in pastry shell. Bake at 350 degrees for 40 to 50 minutes, or until knife inserted near center comes out clean.

Makes 6 to 8 servings.

4
Bake and Give

There is a wonderful, inviting warmth that radiates from the kitchen during the holidays. The evidence of Christmas preparation is everywhere . . . baking, greeting cards being made, notes and lists pinned on the bulletin board, children's holiday art taped to the refrigerator, bundles of food, gifts waiting to be wrapped, and tree ornaments yet to be hung. And the kitchen is often the center of holiday socializing and the place where family and friends can meet to exchange greetings or make holiday plans. To enjoy a warm cup of cider with friends, place a saucepan filled with cider, cinnamon, cloves, and orange peel on the range, let it simmer, and the aroma will invite your guests directly into the kitchen for an informal luncheon or a Christmas brunch. Moreover, the kitchen offers plenty of working space needed for a productive baking party.

If you choose to make edible gifts from the kitchen, then turn the activity into a party. Many of the most successful gifts are also the easiest to make, and there's no reason you can't do this with friends. Midmorning is often a convenient time to gather a few friends for a couple of hours of baking, wrapping, and of course, exchanging holiday recipes. Or perhaps after dinner, invite some friends to help bake cookies. It's fun to work together and have a sweet payoff. Another unusual party time could be before breakfast. The fresh-baked fruit breads can be wrapped and nibbled while drinking coffee at breakfast.

A kitchen party or baking workshop brings people together in a comfortable surrounding that ensures lots of conversation, exchanging of ideas, and perhaps some bake-and-give gifts ready to be carried home.

Wrapping Holiday Edibles

Getting ready for Christmas often means a kitchen filled with the aroma of freshly baked cookies, breads, and cakes, brandied fruits, and the fragrance of blended spices and herbs. But no matter how wonderful these foods look and smell, the art of wrapping must capture their freshness and present each homemade edible as a personal gift.

Wrapping Cookies

One of the nicest things about Christmas cookies is their special holiday appearance. Cookies should be packaged in airtight wrapping or containers if they aren't going to be eaten immediately. Place them in pretty tins or fancy boxes; for a special effect, cluster a few cookies on top of a wrapped gift or as ornaments on a tree. A simple festive presentation is to cover the cookies with cellophane by bringing together all of the edges and tightly sealing with a satin ribbon. Another wonderful gift is the traditional basket of Christmas cookies lined with doilies and fabric—fill it with a variety of such cookies as large gingerbread animals or geese nested on top, and tie it together with a large satin bow. This is the ultimate holiday bake-and-give gift that will be received with much enthusiasm and appreciation. Instructions for baking these cookies are on pages 154–55.

Breads as Gifts

Breads are wonderful items to have on hand during the holidays, and they are doubly welcomed as gifts. Because breads can be baked in a variety of pans and the holidays are synonymous with fancy packaging, don't overlook the possibilities of varying the shapes of your holiday baking. Tube pans, fancy molds, small and large loaf pans, and even long, narrow pâté pans produce stunning gift breads. Breads can be baked ahead of time and frozen, which simplifies some of your holiday tasks.

Packing Your Herbs and Spices

Before you blend herbs or mix together spices spend some time finding special containers. Herbed oils can be stored in unusual jars or old bottles that you've collected; fabulous small tins or inexpensive but charming colored paper boxes can be used for spices and potpourri. An intriguing shape always makes gift opening even more fun on Christmas morning. Chinese takeout cartons embellished with ribbons and stickers are inexpensive containers for spice blends. Shown on page 55 are decorated acrylic boxes that are easy to make.

Fruits and Spirits . . .

Fruit packed in glass jars looks elegant and is an easily prepared edible gift. Trim the jars with lacy paper doilies or colored cellophane and tie with bows; make labels from Christmas gift tags. For a very special gift, arrange all of your edible gifts in baskets lined with fabric and trimmed with ribbons or dried flowers.

Homestyle Food Gifts

Beyond the fact that there is little fear of someone else duplicating your gift, and beyond the fact that it usually is considerably less expensive to make your own gifts, there's a wonderful feeling on the part of both giver and receiver when you make your own Christmas gifts.

Whether it's candy cane cookies or a rich fruit bread, a prettily packaged homestyle gift is always appreciated. Many of the most successful gifts of this sort are the easiest. Anyone can tuck a sprig or two of fresh green herbs into a pretty bottle filled with a good olive oil. Or mix up an inspired combination of compatible spices and herbs that will add zest to a friend's meals. Just remember that at this time of year, the packaging is almost as important as the contents.

Spices and herb blends

Herb-flavored vinegars and oils, when bottled at home, are thoughtful gifts

54

They look professional, yet these acetate spice boxes are easy to make

Peppery Basil Vinegar

1 quart white or red wine vinegar
3 or 4 long sprigs fresh basil
10 black peppercorns

Pour vinegar into a decorative bottle or a jar with a tight-fitting cap. Add the basil and peppercorns, being careful to keep basil sprigs whole. Cap and let stand in a cool, dark place for several weeks to develop flavor.

Makes 1 quart.

Tarragon Vinegar

1 quart white wine vinegar
6 sprigs fresh tarragon

Pour vinegar into a decorative bottle or a jar with a tight-fitting cap. Add the tarragon sprigs, being careful to keep them intact. Cap and let stand in a cool, dark place for several weeks to develop flavor.

Makes 1 quart.

Herbed Oil

1 cup olive oil
3 or 4 sprigs fresh rosemary
1 sprig fresh thyme
2 bay leaves
3 cloves garlic, peeled and halved

Pour the oil into a decorative bottle or a jar with a tight-fitting cap. Add the rosemary and thyme, being careful to keep sprigs whole. Add the bay leaves and garlic. Cover and let stand at room temperature for several days. Store in a cool, dry place. Use in salad dressings, marinades, or as a baste for poultry.

Makes 1 cup.

Italian Herb Mixture

3 tablespoons dried crushed oregano
2 tablespoons dried crushed basil leaves
2 tablespoons dried crushed marjoram
2 tablespoons dried parsley flakes
1 tablespoon fennel seeds
1 tablespoon crushed thyme
1 tablespoon dried rosemary leaves
2 small bay leaves, finely crumbled

Combine oregano, basil, marjoram, parsley, fennel seeds, thyme, rosemary, and bay leaves, and toss to blend. Store in a tightly sealed jar away from light. Use as needed to season soups, stews, and spaghetti sauces.

Makes about ¾ cup.

Pickling Spice Mixture

4 cinnamon sticks, crushed
1 1-inch piece ginger root, peeled and shredded
2 tablespoons mustard seeds
2 teaspoons whole allspice berries
2 tablespoons black peppercorns
2 teaspoons whole cloves
2 teaspoons dill seeds
2 teaspoons whole coriander seeds
2 teaspoons whole mace, crumbled
8 bay leaves, crumbled
1 small dried hot red pepper, crushed, or ¼
    teaspoon crushed red pepper

Combine cinnamon, ginger, mustard seeds, allspice, peppercorns, cloves, dill seeds, coriander seeds, mace, bay leaves, and red pepper, and toss to blend. Store in a tightly sealed jar and shake to mix well before using.

Makes about ⅔ cup.

Orange-Glazed Pear-Nut Bread

1 (16-ounce) can pear halves
1½ cups all-purpose flour
¾ cup granulated sugar
1 tablespoon baking powder
1 teaspoon salt
¼ teaspoon ground allspice
1 cup whole wheat flour
¼ cup oil
1 egg, beaten
1 tablespoon grated orange peel
1 cup chopped walnuts
Orange Glaze

Drain pears, reserving syrup. Reserve 1 pear half for garnish. Purée remaining pears. Add reserved syrup to puréed pears to measure 1 cup. Sift together all-purpose flour, granulated sugar, baking powder, salt, and allspice. Stir in whole wheat flour. Mix puréed pears with oil, egg, and orange peel. Stir into flour mixture. Blend in nuts. Pour into a greased 9 × 5-inch loaf pan. Cut reserved pear half into 6 lengthwise slices. Arrange over top of batter. Bake at 350 degrees for 50 to 55 minutes, or until cake tester inserted near center comes out clean. Cool in pan 10 minutes, then turn out onto cake rack to cool. Spoon glaze over cooled bread. Let bread set overnight before slicing.

Orange Glaze
2 to 3 tablespoons orange juice
1½ to 1¾ cups powdered sugar

Blend orange juice and powdered sugar to make glaze.

Makes 1 loaf.

Pineapple-Zucchini Bread

3 eggs
1 cup oil
2 cups sugar
2 teaspoons vanilla
2 cups coarsely shredded zucchini, drained
1 (8-ounce) can crushed pineapple, drained well
3 cups flour
2 teaspoons baking soda
1 teaspoon salt
½ teaspoon baking powder
1½ teaspoons ground cinnamon
¾ teaspoon ground nutmeg
1 cup finely chopped nuts or mixture of chopped
   nuts and raisins

Beat eggs lightly with a rotary mixer. Add oil, sugar, and vanilla. Continue beating until thick and foamy. Stir in zucchini and pineapple. In another bowl, combine flour, soda, salt, baking powder, cinnamon, nutmeg, and nuts. Stir gently into zucchini mixture just until blended. Divide batter equally between 2 greased and floured 9 × 5-inch loaf pans. Bake at 350 degrees for 1 hour, or until cake tester inserted near center comes out clean. Cool in pans 10 minutes, then turn out onto cake racks to cool thoroughly.

Makes 2 loaves.

The makings for Christmas gifts of food

Cellophane, doilies, and pretty ribbons gracefully decorate homemade fruit preserves

59

Christmas Cutouts

1 cup butter or margarine, softened
1 cup sifted powdered sugar
½ teaspoon salt
2 cups sifted flour
1 cup finely chopped almonds
1 cup oats
2 (1-ounce) squares semisweet chocolate,
    melted and cooled
2 tablespoons crushed peppermint candy

Cream butter and powdered sugar together until light. Stir in salt. Gradually add the flour and almonds to creamed mixture, stirring well after each addition. Stir in oats. Divide dough in half. Add melted chocolate to one half and peppermint candy to the other half. Chill dough for 20 minutes.

On surface dusted with powdered sugar, roll out chocolate dough to a thickness of ⅛-inch. Cut out cookies with holiday cutters dipped in sugar. Using a small cutter, cut smaller cookies from dough scraps to use as centers for larger cookies. Repeat with peppermint dough. Place chocolate centers on large peppermint cookies and peppermint centers on large chocolate cookies. Bake on ungreased baking sheets at 350 degrees for 8 to 10 minutes. Remove to wire racks to cool.

Makes 5 to 8 dozen.

Candy Cane Cookies

1 cup butter or margarine, softened
1 cup sifted powdered sugar
1 egg
1½ teaspoons almond extract
1 teaspoon vanilla
2¾ cups sifted flour
½ teaspoon salt
½ teaspoon red food coloring

Mix butter, powdered sugar, egg, almond extract, and vanilla, blending thoroughly. Sift flour and salt together and stir into butter mixture. Divide dough in half and blend food coloring into one half. Divide each half into four parts. Cover separately with plastic wrap and chill thoroughly. When chilled, remove 1 part red dough and 1 part white dough at a time from refrigerator. Measuring 2 rounded teaspoons dough for each strip of dough, roll dough on lightly floured board into 4-inch-long fingers. Place red and white strips side by side, press lightly together, and then twist like ropes. Place strips on ungreased baking sheets, curving one end around to form a cane handle. Bake at 375 degrees for about 9 minutes or until lightly browned. If desired, sprinkle warm cookies with a mixture of finely crushed peppermint candy and sugar.

Makes about 3 dozen cookies.

Note: This is a very soft dough, so for best results roll out strips for only 1 cookie at a time and complete the cookie before starting a second one.

Lacy English Gingersnaps

1 cup flour
¼ cup butter or margarine
1 cup light brown sugar, packed
1½ teaspoons ground ginger
5 tablespoons dark or light corn syrup

Cut flour and butter together with a pastry blender until crumbly. Add the brown sugar and ginger. Stir in syrup to make a stiff dough. Pinch off marble-size pieces of dough and place far apart on well-greased baking sheets. Bake at 350 degrees for 10 to 15 minutes or until done. Cookies will be thin and lacy when done.

Makes about 10 dozen.

Five-Week Potpourri

¾ cup drained, chopped, canned pineapple
¾ cup drained, chopped, canned peaches or
    apricots
6 maraschino cherries, chopped
1½ cups sugar
1 envelope dry yeast

Place pineapple, peaches, cherries, sugar, and yeast in a clean 2-quart container. Stir mixture well and cover. Set in a cool, dry spot. After first day, stir mixture 3 or 4 times during the next two weeks.
Third Week:
Add 1 cup chopped pineapple or well-drained fruit cocktail and 1 cup sugar to mixture. Stir every other day.
Fourth Week:
Add 1 cup chopped peaches, apricots, or well-drained fruit cocktail and 1 cup sugar to mixture. Stir every other day.
Fifth Week:
Add 1 cup chopped maraschino cherries or well-drained fruit cocktail and 1 cup sugar.
Use mixture as wished, but to keep starter going, add more fruit and sugar approximately every two weeks. When ready to serve, brandy, rum, or bourbon may be added to taste, if desired. Serve as a sauce over pound or sponge cake or ice cream.

Makes about 2 quarts.

5 · A Children's Holiday Workshop

The week before Christmas is the perfect opportunity to channel your children's energy into holiday projects. Simple projects can become treasured gifts if talented young designers are provided with the materials, work area, and time to finish a project.

The Children's Holiday Workshop is a party for a small group or a large gathering when there are enough adults willing to coordinate and supervise. Children are terrific innovators so the projects should be flexible with lots of area for creativity. The best results at the workshop come from children who choose one or two projects to spend their time on.

Lay out all of the materials necessary for each project and have a finished one to display. Be sure to choose projects that guarantee a certain amount of success.

Winter Wreaths

Children of any age like to make wreaths. Aside from actually making the wreaths, a nature walk to collect materials can be part of the workshop. The supplies you'll need include cardboard wreath shapes in desired sizes that must be cut ahead of time. Use pine needles laced with raffia or yarn to decoratively frame an array of pine cones, pods, dried flowers, and ribbons. Glue with heavy craft glue and create the wreath's design using the largest pine cone pieces first, adding smaller dried flowers and pods until the frame is completely covered. Use wire that can be easily pushed through the cardboard, thus making a hook for hanging your wreath.

Clay Necklaces

Clay necklaces are gifts to be given at any time of the year. We used Fimo modeling clay but any similar modeling clay that can be baked will do. Before the clay is rolled into beads, cut the material into cubes. This helps to make the beads consistent in size. The necklaces pictured here have about fifty $\frac{1}{2}$-inch-diameter beads and shapes. Knead the clay until it is very workable. If little shapes are difficult to form, try small cookie cutters and different colored clays layered together. Using a large needle, make holes through your various shapes and beads. Test your materials on a few beads before baking a whole batch of beads. After following the baking instructions for your particular brand of clay, allow the beads to cool, then thread them together on an elastic string.

Garlands

Garlands can be used for trimming a tree, adorning a mantle, bordering a doorway, or decorating a large gift. Anything stringable can be used, and it's a perfect project for younger children. Look for unusual things to string. We tried all kinds of objects: popcorn, cranberries, small wooden toys, bells, plastic horns, candy, beads, sequins, and even small straw baskets.

Yarn Balls

These Christmas ornaments can be as colorful as a child's imagination. The required materials are yarns that vary in color, weight, and texture, lightweight cardboard, yarn needles, and polyester fiberfill.

Cut lightweight cardboard into circles. The large circles should be five inches in diameter, medium, four inches, and small, three inches. With a pencil mark the edge of the circle into twenty-three sections. Notch each section slightly with scissors. String the yarn in the notches on both sides of the circle, covering the pencil marks. Secure the woven web with a knot.

Working from the center, weave a strand of yarn over and under the webbed pattern on both sides of the circle. Alternate colors as desired, securing each section of yarn with a knot. When the entire circle is covered with yarn on both sides, carefully remove the paper circle by cutting out small paper pieces, taking care not to cut the yarn. Stuff with polyester fiberfill, shaping the form into a ball.

Once you've set up the workshop kids take over, whether it's making these small wreaths from natural materials such as pinecones and seeds, or cutting clay shapes for necklaces with small cookie cutters

The finished project: Fimo clay necklaces with charming little shapes

Glass beads, trinkets, and small ornaments are ideal for making garlands

67

Angels and Hobbyhorses

Angels and hobbyhorses on sticks are for the more adventurous. A wood dowel and a pattern cut from felt are the preparations needed before work can begin. There is no limit to the variety of materials that can be used; consider scraps of fabric, glitter, sequins, lace—or anything you've been saving. Patterns for the angels and horse are on pages 150–51 along with instructions for making both projects.

Window Ornaments

These plastic window ornaments form a prism of color when hung on the tree or in front of a window. The project begins with plastic baking crystals that are available in many hobby and craft stores, metal cookie cutters, and small cake forms.

Place the metal forms on aluminum foil or on a cookie sheet. Pour some plastic crystals into the metal forms. Follow baking instructions on packaging and bake just long enough for crystals to melt slightly together to produce a crystalline appearance. Before ornaments are completely cooled, make a small hole in each and insert a thread for hanging.

Cats, Cats, Cats

As a first sewing experience or a perfect project for several children to work together on as a team, this toy cat can be sewn by one child, turned right-side out by another, and perhaps stuffed with fiberfill by a third. Make three cats so that everyone can enjoy sewing eyes, whiskers, and the finishing yarn collar onto their own cat. Please make sure that buttons are sewn on tightly so that children aren't able to pull them off.

Rubber Stamps

For cards, gift wrap, or any personal signature, rubber stamps are an easy, charming solution. Children delight in having their own name carved into a personal plastic eraser stamp. Be sure to assist any younger children who may want to cut their own personal stamp with an X-Acto knife. Poster paints can be used rather than an ink pad, and other materials such as felt markers, crayons, and colored papers can add to the colorful arrangement.

Cookies That Walk Away

Children love to bake and decorate cookies so we designed cookies with that in mind. You'll find a gingerbread boy and girl to make, as well as a cat. The fun is having lots of sugary delights to add and colored frosting to use as cookie glue. We made bases for our cookies and wrapped them in cellophane and ribbons; the instructions are on pages 154–57.

Recipes for Young Cooks, and Their Mothers, Too

Kids love the hoopla that goes with the holiday season, particularly the sweets that are so much a part of any Christmas activity. Nothing could please a hard-working crew of young workers celebrating the completion of whatever Christmas project they are involved with than a frothy glass of peppermint-flavored eggnog and their own special edible snowman. Just be sure to warn them about the skewers that are holding their snowmen together.

69

A lesson in weaving

Materials for yarn balls result in these colored yarn balls, below

Three girls are better than one when it comes to deciding how to decorate the little angel stick toys

Hobbyhorses and angel stick toys

Window ornaments made of baking crystals (above) can be shaped with cake molds (below)

A personal signature stamp made from a plastic eraser

A rubber stamp poster is more interesting when you use different colored stamp pads

73

Roly-Poly Snowmen

Vanilla ice cream
Flake coconut
Sugar cookies
Raisins, chocolate chips, red hots for decoration

For each snowman, scoop 3 different-sized balls of ice cream. Place on a baking sheet and freeze until hard. When very solid, roll ice cream balls in flake coconut to cover well. Place largest ice cream ball on a cookie. Run a bamboo skewer through both the cookie base and ice cream ball. Thread medium ice cream ball on skewer and top with a small one. Return to freezer to freeze hard again. Remove from freezer and decorate: raisins for buttons, chocolate chips for the eyes, and red hots for the nose and mouth. Refreeze up to 1 week. Additional decorations such as tiny paper top hats, Christmas bows, and yarn scarfs may be added, if desired.

Peppermint Nog

6 eggs, separated
½ cup sugar
1 quart milk
¼ teaspoon salt
2 cups whipping cream
½ to 1 teaspoon peppermint extract
Peppermint candy canes for garnish

Beat egg yolks until light. Add ¼ cup of the sugar and beat until sugar is dissolved. Scald milk and stir slowly into egg yolks. Place mixture over low heat and cook, stirring, until mixture coats metal spoon. Chill thoroughly. Several hours before serving, add salt to the egg whites and beat until soft peaks form. Gradually add remaining ¼ cup sugar and continue to beat until stiff peaks form. Fold into custard mixture. Whip cream and fold into eggnog along with peppermint extract. Chill several hours. Ladle into glasses, mugs, or punch cups to serve and garnish with candy canes and additional whipped cream, if desired.

Makes 8 to 16 servings.

Cats, cats, cats, and Kitty

Making Noah's Ark

When God called upon Noah to build an ark, His instructions were fairly explicit. The three-story vessel was to be made of gopherwood, have a window and a door, and its dimensions were to be 300 cubits long, 50 cubits wide, and 30 cubits high (about 450 feet by 75 feet by 45 feet). Once construction was completed, the next step was filling the passenger list. Noah, his wife, his sons, and his sons' wives satisfied the human quota, to be accompanied by an animal kingdom contingent. Specifically, " . . . of every living thing of all flesh, two of every sort shalt thou bring into the ark, to keep them alive with thee: they shall be male and female."

Like the Nativity, Noah's ark is a favorite religious symbol for the holidays. Designed to become a family keepsake, our Noah's Ark can be started this year and animals can be added in the years to come. It can be made from plywood or cardboard and the menageries can be a few simple animals or a jungle of exotic beasts. The ark is also designed for easy storage. Instructions and patterns are on pages 158–63.

Delicious Desserts
for Friends

Once assembled, use your Noah's Ark as a charming centerpiece for your table, graced on either side by some delicious desserts. Invite friends over for a party of sweets and different types of holiday punch. And make sure at least one of the punches is nonalcoholic. Start as much preparation as possible well in advance of the date and rely heavily on your freezer.

It pays to be clever about your menu choices for this type of party. For instance, a showy big trifle made of sherry-sprinkled sponge cake layered with a creamy custard sauce and topped with dollops of whipped cream actually takes less time to prepare and will go a lot farther than tiny individual fruit tarts. In contrast to the light trifle, we've included a substantial fruitcake-like steamed persimmon pudding that is a favorite of Mrs. Reagan. Place one of these pretty holiday treats in the center of a large platter and surround it with thin slices of a second pudding. It won't take much to satisfy any sweet-hungry guest when dolloped with a spoonful of brandy-flavored whipped cream. There are brownies, too, with a sweetened cream cheese filling, and a big meringue filled with chocolate mousse. With this much to choose from, any guest will be appreciative.

Mrs. Reagan's Persimmon Pudding

1 cup sugar
½ cup butter, melted
1 cup flour, sifted
¼ teaspoon salt
1 teaspoon ground cinnamon
1 teaspoon ground nutmeg
1 cup puréed persimmon pulp (3 to 4 very
    ripe fruits)
2 teaspoons baking soda
2 teaspoons warm water
Brandy
1 teaspoon vanilla
2 eggs, lightly beaten
1 cup raisins
½ cup chopped walnuts, optional
Brandy Whipped Cream Sauce

Stir together the sugar and melted butter. Re-sift flour with the salt, cinnamon, and nutmeg. Add to butter mixture. Add persimmon pulp, baking soda dissolved in the warm water, 3 table-spoons brandy, and vanilla. Add eggs, mixing lightly but thoroughly. Add raisins and nuts, stirring just until mixed.

Turn into a buttered 5- to 6-cup heatproof mold. Cover and place on rack in kettle. Pour in enough boiling water to reach halfway up the sides of mold. Cover kettle and simmer for 2½ to 3 hours. Let stand a few minutes, then unmold onto warm serving dish. Pour about ¼ cup warmed brandy over pudding and flame. Serve with Brandy Whipped Cream Sauce.

Makes 6 to 8 servings.

Brandy Whipped Cream Sauce
1 egg
⅓ cup butter, melted
1 cup sifted powdered sugar
Pinch salt
1 tablespoon brandy flavoring
1 cup whipping cream, whipped

Beat egg until light and fluffy. Beat in butter, sugar, salt, and brandy flavoring. Gently fold whipped cream into mixture. Cover and chill.

Christmas Trifle

4 eggs, separated
½ cup sugar
1 cup milk
Pinch salt
1 teaspoon vanilla
1 (8-inch) round sponge cake
¼ cup sherry
1 (10-ounce) jar raspberry jam
Whipped cream
Strawberries, halved

Blend egg yolks and sugar in top of double boiler. Stir in milk and salt and place over hot water. Cook, stirring, until custard coats a metal spoon. Remove from hot water and stir in vanilla. Cool, stirring occasionally. Beat egg whites until stiff and fold into cooled custard.

Split sponge cake and place one layer in bottom of deep 8-inch glass dish. Sprinkle with 2 tablespoons sherry and spread with half the jam. Top with second layer and repeat process, using remaining sherry and jam. Pour cooled custard over cake and chill for 1 hour. Garnish with whipped cream and strawberries.

Makes 6 to 8 servings.

Christmas Trifle

Holiday Tea Punch

OPPOSITE *Mrs. Reagan's Persimmon Pudding served with Brandy Whipped Cream Sauce*

Cream Cheese-Filled Brownies

5 1-ounce squares unsweetened chocolate
1¼ cups butter or margarine
5 eggs
3 cups sugar
1 teaspoon salt
2 teaspoons vanilla
2 cups sifted flour
⅔ cup coarsely chopped walnuts
2 8-ounce packages cream cheese, softened
Maraschino cherries, drained
Walnut halves

Melt chocolate with butter. In a large bowl beat the eggs, 2½ cups of the sugar, salt, and vanilla. Add melted chocolate mixture. Mix until blended. Add flour gradually while beating on low speed. Mix in nuts. Turn into greased and wax paper-lined (18 × 12-inch) baking tray, spreading mixture evenly. Bake at 350 degrees for about 20 minutes, being careful not to overbake. Cool. Remove from tray. Slice in half crosswise to obtain 2 layers.

Beat cream cheese until smooth. Beat in remaining ½ cup sugar until smooth. Set aside ⅓ cup mixture. Spread remaining cream cheese mixture on one layer of brownies. Top with second brownie layer. Cut into 15 servings and top each with dollop of reserved cream cheese and garnish with drained maraschino cherry or walnut half.

Makes 15 brownies.

Chocolate Mousse Pie

Chocolate Meringue Shell
1 envelope unflavored gelatin
½ cup sugar
¼ teaspoon salt
1 teaspoon instant coffee powder or crystals
3 eggs, separated
1 cup milk
3 1-ounce squares unsweetened chocolate
½ teaspoon vanilla
¼ teaspoon cream of tartar
1 cup whipping cream, whipped
White chocolate, melted
Strawberries

Prepare Chocolate Meringue Shell. Then, mix gelatin, ¼ cup of the sugar, salt, and coffee in large, heavy saucepan. Beat egg yolks. Blend in milk and beaten egg yolks. Break chocolate into smaller pieces and add. Heat slowly until chocolate is melted and mixture slightly thickened. Do not boil. Pour into large bowl, stir in vanilla, and cool until mixture mounds.

Beat egg whites with cream of tartar until foamy. Beat in remaining ¼ cup sugar 1 tablespoon at a time and continue beating until stiff peaks form. Beat cooled chocolate mixture until smooth. Fold in egg whites, then whipped cream. Pour into prepared Chocolate Meringue Shell. Chill until firm, about 4 hours. Top with strawberries dipped in melted white chocolate.

Makes 10 to 12 servings.

Note: This pie is not very sweet. If desired, add up to ½ cup sugar, dividing sugar equally between egg yolks and whites, for more sweetness.

Chocolate Meringue Shell
5 egg whites
¼ teaspoon cream of tartar
1⅔ cups sugar
½ cup powdered cocoa

Beat egg whites with cream of tartar until frothy. Gradually add sugar, beating until stiff and glossy. Sprinkle with cocoa, folding until blended. Line baking sheet or pizza pan with brown paper. Turn meringue mixture into brown paper, shaping it into a 9-inch round shell and building up sides. Bake at 275 degrees for 45 minutes. Turn off oven; leave meringue in oven until cool. Store at room temperature until serving time.

Passion Punch

3 cups pineapple juice
¾ cup passion fruit nectar
¾ cup orgeat syrup
¾ cup grenadine
Juice of 6 limes
2 (1-liter) bottles club soda

Combine pineapple juice, passion fruit nectar, orgeat and grenadine syrups, and lime juice, and chill well. At serving time, stir in club soda and pour mixture over ice in a large punch bowl.

Makes about 30 punch cup servings.

Sparkling Punch

1 (12-ounce) can frozen lemonade concentrate, thawed
1 cup fresh orange juice
1 quart bourbon or light rum
1 (8-ounce) jar maraschino cherries
2 (1-liter) bottles ginger ale
1 orange, thinly sliced

Combine lemonade concentrate, orange juice, bourbon, and cherries, and chill well. At serving time stir in ginger ale and pour mixture over ice in punch bowl. Garnish with orange slices.

Makes about 24 punch cup servings.

OVERLEAF *Top row, right: Chocolate Mousse Pie; bottom right: Cream Cheese-Filled Brownies*

Holiday Tea Punch

⅓ cup instant tea powder
2 cups water
1 cup grenadine
2 cups cranberry juice cocktail
2 (6-ounce) cans pineapple juice
1 (6-ounce) can frozen limeade concentrate,
    thawed
2 tablespoons lemon juice
3 (12-ounce) cans lemon-lime carbonated beverage
Fruited Ice Ring

Combine tea powder, water, grenadine, cranberry juice cocktail, pineapple juice, limeade, and lemon juice. Stir to blend well. Chill thoroughly. At serving time, stir in carbonated beverage and pour over Fruited Ice Ring in punch bowl.

Makes about 20 punch cup servings.

Fruited Ice Ring
Water
1 small orange
Sliced strawberries, seedless grapes, or well-
    drained pineapple chunks

Fill a 6-cup mold halfway with water and freeze. Peel orange and separate into segments. When water in mold is frozen, remove from freezer, add about ¼-inch more water and arrange orange segments and strawberries or other fruit attractively in mold. Return to freezer. When fruit is frozen, remove from freezer and fill mold to top. Freeze hard. To unmold, dip mold briefly in hot water and turn out into punch bowl.

An attractive holiday setting

Staging a Portrait Party

A unique idea for those with children that will make an open house during the Christmas season more fun than usual is a party that includes Santa as the guest of honor. Children will love sitting on his lap and having their pictures taken. Plus, you'll enjoy not having to wait in line in a department store to visit Santa, and by staging the party at home, there are some delicious buffet foods you can serve. The portrait party and the buffet require some extra work on your part, so give yourself a few weeks to plan ahead. Recruit a likely Santa from friends or family members. If you don't want to rent a costume, make one. The traditional red suit can be sewn easily with some red flannel; for fun sew bells on the suit or on Santa's white gloves, and add fur trim to his suit, cap, and black rubber boots. And if your Santa needs some "stuffing" add that, too, and the necessary wide black belt. Makeup should include rouge for cheeks and nose, a bit of white powder for the hairline and brow, and a touch of mascara. Don't forget a softly curled beard and wig, gold-rimmed spectacles without reflective glass, and a touch of holly on the cap. Have some paper and pencil for making lists of the children's requests.

Set a "stage" for Santa and the children with lots of holiday color . . . a Christmas tree, strings of lights or festive garlands, maybe a wreath over the fireplace. The focal point should be Santa sitting in a chair with colorfully wrapped gifts and toys surrounding him.

Select a few amateur photographers in your group to set up the shooting sessions, which should be about ten or fifteen minutes apart. Place the tripod to take advantage of any natural light in the room and position Santa so that he and his visitors are not directly facing the lens, thus avoiding the glare from flash bulbs. For close-up shots, place the camera five to seven feet away from Santa and use a 50 to 55 mm lens. Otherwise, choose a spot about ten to twelve feet away. Keep your eye open and your camera ready for the unexpected tears and shy glances that children have been known to greet Santa with.

Planning a buffet during holidays is always an ambitious undertaking, and works best with a certain amount of compromise. There is little time to experiment on exotic recipes, so rely on delicious, familiar foods that can be prepared in advance and refrigerated, or frozen, then reheated in the oven or microwave at the last minute. Spectacular, tasty desserts are always welcome at a party, and if you want some holiday punch, keep in mind there are always those who prefer something nonalcoholic. All of the recipes we've included will make a perfect buffet for you.

Traditional Roast Beef Feast

Jellied Consommé
Standing Beef Rib Roast
Horseradish Cream, Beef Gravy
Yorkshire Pudding
Vegetable Casserole with Cheese Sauce

or

Stuffed Acorn Squash
Marinated Broccoli and Grapefruit
Raspberry Aspic
Braised Cucumbers in Dill Sauce
Assorted Relishes   Hot Rolls and Butter
Your Favorite Dessert
Coffee or Tea

Standing Beef Rib Roast

Select a rib roast of prime or choice grade. Wipe lightly with a dampened paper towel. Sprinkle with coarse salt and season with fresh, coarsely ground pepper. Rub salt and pepper well into all surfaces. Allow roast to come to room temperature. Place roast, fat side up, curved side of ribs down, in a shallow pan so that ribs hold meat above drippings. (A rack may be used, but usually isn't necessary when ribs are on bottom.)

Insert a meat thermometer into thickest part of roast, making sure it doesn't touch the bone. Cook meat at 325 degrees until thermometer registers 130 to 140 degrees for rare, 140 to 150 degrees for medium, or 160 to 170 degrees for well done. Cooking time can only be estimated. A thermometer is a better guide to doneness.

Use the following times as a guideline only: 1¼ to 2⅓ hours for a 4-pound roast; 2¼ to 3⅓ hours for a 6-pound roast; 3 to 4½ hours for an 8-pound roast; 4½ to 5 hours for a 10-pound roast, and 5 to 5½ hours for a 13-pound roast.

Horseradish Cream

2 cups whipping cream
1 tablespoon sugar
¼ cup drained, prepared white horseradish

Combine whipping cream, sugar, and horseradish in deep bowl. Blend well and chill at least 2 hours. Just before serving, whip cream mixture until soft peaks form. Serve with roast beef.

Makes about 4 cups.

Yorkshire Pudding

4 eggs
2 cups milk
1½ cups flour
Pinch salt
½ cup beef drippings or oil

Beat eggs until light and fluffy. Beat in milk and flour, alternating small amounts at a time. Add salt and 2 tablespoons drippings. Divide remaining 6 tablespoons drippings between 2 8-inch square baking pans. Heat pans with drippings at 450 degrees until drippings are very hot. Remove from oven and pour half of batter into each pan. Return pans to oven and bake for 10 to 15 minutes, or until pudding is puffy and golden brown.

Makes about 8 servings.

Standing Beef Rib Roast and trimmings

Marinated Broccoli and Grapefruit

95

OPPOSITE *Capture a special moment on film*

Vegetable Casserole

4 ears corn, kernels cut from cob, or 2 (10-ounce)
    packages frozen whole kernel corn
1½ cups fresh peas or 1 (10-ounce) package
    frozen tiny peas
1 medium head cauliflower, broken into flowerets
1 bunch green onions, trimmed and sliced
1 cup sliced celery
1½ cups green beans, cut into 1-inch pieces
Salted water
1 (10 ¾-ounce) can condensed cream of chicken
    soup, undiluted
⅓ cup milk
Salt, pepper
1 cup shredded Swiss cheese

Combine corn, peas, cauliflower, onions, celery, and green beans in a large saucepan. Cover with salted water and simmer until vegetables are barely tender, about 20 minutes. Drain well. Keep warm. Heat chicken soup and milk in saucepan. Season to taste with salt and pepper. Stir in cheese and heat until cheese melts. To serve, place vegetables in serving bowl and serve hot sauce on side.

Makes about 8 servings.

Variation: If desired, cooked vegetables may be placed in a 2-quart casserole and heated sauce poured over them. Bake at 350 degrees for about 30 minutes or until mixture is heated through.

Stuffed Acorn Squash

3 medium acorn squash
3 cups *Quick Rice Pilaf*
1 cup cottage cheese
¼ cup minced green onions or chives
2 eggs, beaten
Melted butter or margarine
12 4-inch-long strips thinly sliced Cheddar cheese

Pierce whole squash in 3 or 4 places with metal skewer. Cook on *high* in microwave oven for 8 minutes per pound, turning as needed according to oven manufacturer's directions. Wrap squash in foil and let stand in warm spot for 7 to 10 minutes. Discard foil. Cut squash in half lengthwise and remove seeds. Fill each half with mixture of Quick Rice Pilaf, cottage cheese, green onions, and eggs. Brush melted butter over exposed surfaces of squash. Place squash in microwave and cook on *high* for 3 minutes. Place 2 strips Cheddar cheese over each squash half, return to oven, and cook on *high* for 1 minute.

Makes 6 servings.

Quick Rice Pilaf
2 cups water
2 tablespoons butter or margarine
4 teaspoons chicken bouillon
2 teaspoons minced onion
2 cups instant rice

Combine water, butter, bouillon, and onion in a deep casserole. Cover and microwave on *high* for 3 minutes or until mixture comes to a boil. Remove from oven, stir in rice, cover tightly, and let stand 7 to 10 minutes or until rice has absorbed liquid.

Marinated Broccoli and Grapefruit

1 grapefruit, peeled and sectioned
2 pounds broccoli, cleaned and trimmed
1 cup bottled Italian dressing
1/4 cup pitted ripe olives, for garnish
1 tablespoon pimiento strips, for garnish

Place grapefruit sections in a bowl, reserving the juice. Refrigerate grapefruit. Split stems of broccoli if more than 1-inch thick. Steam broccoli over boiling water until barely tender. Drain and place in a shallow glass dish. Combine Italian dressing and 1/4 cup of the reserved grapefruit juice. Pour mixture over hot broccoli, cover, and chill until very cold, at least 2 hours. Chill olives and pimiento. At serving time, arrange broccoli spears on platter, add grapefruit sections, and garnish with olives and pimiento.

Makes about 6 servings.

Raspberry Aspic

2 (3-ounce) packages raspberry gelatin
3/4 cup hot water
2 (1-pound) cans stewed tomatoes
Hot pepper sauce

Dissolve gelatin in hot water. Place stewed tomatoes and their liquid in blender container and blend just until coarsely chopped. Add to gelatin along with 3 or 4 drops of hot pepper sauce. Turn mixture into a lightly oiled 2-quart mold and chill until firm. To serve, unmold on a bed of greens, if desired, and serve mayonnaise on the side.

Makes about 8 servings.

Braised Cucumbers in Dill Sauce

6 medium cucumbers
1/4 cup butter or margarine
Salt, pepper
Dill Sauce

Peel cucumbers and cut in half lengthwise. Scoop out and discard seeds. Cut cucumbers in 1-inch chunks. Melt butter in a 2-quart saucepan over low heat. Add cucumbers and toss to coat with butter. Cover saucepan and simmer gently for 10 minutes. Remove from heat and season to taste with salt and pepper. Toss with Dill Sauce and serve warm.

Makes 6 to 8 servings.

Dill Sauce
1/4 cup butter or margarine
2 tablespoons flour
2 teaspoons chicken-seasoned stock base
1 cup warm water
1/4 to 1/2 teaspoon white pepper
Seasoned salt
2 cups sour cream
1 tablespoon minced fresh dill weed or 1 teaspoon
   dried dill weed

Melt butter in a small saucepan over low heat. Blend in flour and cook, stirring, for 1 to 2 minutes. Stir in stock base and warm water. Add white pepper and continue to cook and stir until mixture thickens. Remove from heat and season to taste with seasoned salt. Stir in sour cream and dill weed. Heat over low heat but do not allow to boil.

Makes about 3 cups sauce.

Raspberry Aspic

Braised Cucumbers in Dill Sauce

98

Stuffed Acorn Squash

Glazed Baked Ham Dinner

Assorted Canapés and Hors d'Oeuvres
Baked Ham with Honey-Berry Glaze
Turkish Eggplant Salad
Sweet Potato Casserole
Sour Cream Raisin Pie
Fred MacMurray's Pumpkin Pie
Coffee   Champagne

Baked Ham with Honey-Berry Glaze

1 (7- to 10-pound) boneless fully cooked ham
Honey-Berry Glaze

Place ham on a rack in an open roasting pan. Insert meat thermometer so it is centered in the thickest part of the ham. Bake ham at 325 degrees until thermometer registers 140 degrees. Allow approximately 15 to 18 minutes per pound. Spread ham generously with Honey-Berry Glaze 20 minutes before end of cooking time. Remove from oven and let stand at least 15 minutes before slicing.

Makes about 20 servings.

Honey-Berry Glaze
1 (14-ounce) jar cranberry-orange relish
¼ cup honey
¼ teaspoon ground cinnamon
¼ teaspoon ground cloves

Combine relish, honey, cinnamon, and cloves in a small saucepan. Cook over low heat for 10 minutes, stirring occasionally.

Turkish Eggplant Salad

2 medium eggplants, halved
2 tablespoons olive oil
2 tablespoons lemon juice
2 tablespoons dry white wine
2 cloves garlic, mashed
1 large green pepper, cored, seeded, and finely chopped
2 cups plain yogurt
Salt, pepper
Pinch dried mint leaves
Pinch dried oregano leaves
Shredded lettuce
Parsley sprigs
Sliced radishes
2 thin slices red onion

Place eggplants, cut side down, on lightly greased baking sheet. Bake at 350 degrees for 45 minutes or until soft. Remove from oven and let cool. Scoop out pulp and mix with olive oil, lemon juice, wine, garlic, green pepper, and yogurt. Season to taste with salt and pepper. Blend in mint and oregano. Cover and chill for several hours or overnight. At serving time, mound eggplant mixture on serving plate. Surround with shredded lettuce and parsley. Sprinkle radish slices over eggplant and top with sliced onion rings.

Makes 8 servings.

Sweet Potato Casserole

4 cups hot, cooked, and mashed sweet potatoes
⅓ cup butter or margarine
2 tablespoons granulated sugar
2 eggs, beaten
½ cup milk
⅓ cup chopped pecans
⅓ cup flake coconut
⅓ cup brown sugar, packed
2 tablespoons flour
2 tablespoons butter, melted

Combine sweet potatoes, butter, and granulated sugar. Beat in eggs and milk. Pour mixture into a 1½- to 2-quart casserole. Combine pecans, coconut, brown sugar, and flour. Stir in the 2 tablespoons melted butter. Sprinkle mixture over sweet potatoes. Bake at 325 degrees for 1 hour.

Makes 6 to 8 servings.

Sour Cream Raisin Pie

2 eggs
¾ cup honey
1 cup sour cream
2 tablespoons sherry or fruit juice
½ teaspoon ground cinnamon
¼ teaspoon salt
2 tablespoons flour
1½ cups raisins
1 unbaked 9-inch pie shell

Beat eggs until thick. Blend honey, sour cream, and sherry. Fold into beaten eggs. Mix cinnamon, salt, and flour with raisins and add to egg mixture. Pour into pie shell and bake at 425 degrees for 10 minutes. Reduce heat to 375 degrees and continue baking for 25 minutes. Cool before cutting.

Makes 6 to 8 servings.

Fred MacMurray's Pumpkin Pie

1⅔ cups crushed gingersnaps
¼ cup melted butter
½ cup brown sugar, packed
2 envelopes unflavored gelatin
½ teaspoon salt
½ teaspoon ground cinnamon
¼ teaspoon ground nutmeg
¼ teaspoon ground ginger
1 cup milk
4 eggs, separated
1½ cups canned pumpkin
⅓ cup rum
½ cup granulated sugar
½ cup flake coconut

Mix gingersnap crumbs with butter in a 9-inch pie plate. Press mixture firmly in bottom and around sides of plate. Thoroughly mix brown sugar, gelatin, salt, cinnamon, nutmeg, and ginger in a heavy saucepan. Stir in milk, egg yolks, and pumpkin, blending well. Cook over low heat, stirring frequently, about 10 minutes, until the mixture begins to bubble and the gelatin is completely dissolved. Let cool to room temperature, then stir in rum. Chill mixture until it thickens enough to mound slightly when dropped from a spoon. Beat egg whites until stiff. Beat in granulated sugar a small amount at a time, then beat until smooth. Fold egg whites into pumpkin mixture. Ladle into prepared pie shell and chill until firm, at least 2 hours. Meanwhile spread coconut on baking sheet and bake at 350 degrees for 5 to 10 minutes until browned. Stir once or twice to brown evenly. Sprinkle toasted coconut over pie.

Makes 6 to 8 servings.

8

Trim the Tree Party

Trimming the tree has always been a traditional time to give a party, a special time to gather family and friends. For the more ambitious, a tree-trimming party can begin with making paper ornaments to hang on the tree, or preparing special gift boxes and working with ribbon. Another appealing idea is making your own centerpiece for the table—we've made lots of paper-cut geese as a runner for the holiday table. Otherwise, bringing people together is great for helping with the stringing of lights, carefully unwrapping holiday decorations, and hanging ornaments on the tree.

If You're Papering the House

The materials used to make paper decorations should be selected with some idea of how they are going to be used. The organic structure of paper often determines how it can be used, so choose a paper that best fits the project. You may find a wonderful, colored, plastic-coated paper that's difficult to cut and crease. Sometimes thin gift wrap tears or stains easily, and although heavy tag boards are strong, they seldom are very colorful. A useful rule: Use thin papers for multifolding patterns, and strong paper, such as Strathmore two-ply, for simple cut-and-fold projects. Experiment by combining types of papers, such as cardboard with tissue inserts, or by bonding two thin papers together with spray adhesive. Look for unusual papers and colors, such as paper plates, book covers, recycled cards, and tissues, and watch for foils or plastic papers. In the project section, along with the patterns and instructions for making these crafts, we explain more about the materials you need, and give a few tips as well.

Do-It-Yourself Omelets

We suggest having your guests prepare their own dinner, which keeps the atmosphere informal and no doubt will satisfy any appetite. The do-it-yourself omelet solves the food problem and doesn't require a lot of time or attention. Provide a chafing dish or small electric omelet pan and decoratively set a table with a variety of fillings for the omelets. Almost anything goes, so we've given choices from a classic ham and cheese filling to shrimps with garlic butter. Add baskets of croissants or bread, and serve a salad of tomatoes and fresh basil. There's also a coffee drink for those who want a little "kick." And for dessert, serve a traditional Bûche de Noël, or yule log, especially appropriate for a Christmas tree-trimming party. This you need to make ahead of time—but keep it chilled until you're ready for dessert.

Basic Omelet for Two

4 eggs
¼ cup milk or water
½ teaspoon salt
⅛ teaspoon pepper
1 tablespoon butter or margarine
Filling

Beat eggs until light and frothy. Add milk, salt, and pepper, and beat again. Heat butter in an 8-inch sauté pan over medium heat. Tilt pan so butter covers bottom surface. Pour in egg mixture and cook without stirring until eggs begin to set around edges. Draw set portions of the egg toward center of pan with a fork, allowing uncooked egg to flow to bottom of pan. Tilt pan, if necessary, to disperse liquid part of eggs. When eggs have set and top is creamy, add filling of your choice to one half of omelet and fold other half over it. Slide onto heated serving dish.

Makes 2 servings.

Ten Variations

Cheddar Cheese Filling
For each omelet allow ½ cup shredded Cheddar cheese.

Ham and Cheese Filling
Allow ¼ cup each finely diced cooked ham and shredded Cheddar cheese for each omelet.

Mushroom Filling
Allow ½ cup sliced mushrooms sautéed in 1 teaspoon butter for each omelet.

Cottage Cheese Filling
Allow ¼ cup cottage cheese mixed with 1 tablespoon chopped chives for each omelet.

Shrimp Filling
Allow ¼ cup tiny cooked shrimp for each omelet. Sauté briefly in 1 tablespoon garlic butter. To make garlic butter, sauté 4 mashed cloves garlic in 1 cup butter for 2 to 3 minutes. Discard garlic cloves and use butter to sauté shrimp.

Chicken Liver Filling
Dice chicken livers. Allow about ¼ cup livers per omelet. Sauté briefly in 1 tablespoon butter and 1 tablespoon cream sherry. Add 1 tablespoon chopped green onions, if desired.

Mixed Vegetable Filling
Cook frozen mixed vegetables according to package directions. Drain well. For each omelet, combine ½ cup cooked vegetables with 2 tablespoons canned tomato sauce.

Bacon and Tomato Filling
Crumble cooked bacon with seeded and finely chopped tomatoes. Allow ½ cup mixture per omelet.

Fruit Filling
Spread almost-set omelet with thawed frozen raspberries, strawberries, or other fruits. Allow about ½ cup fruit per omelet. Fold, top with a dollop of sour cream, and sprinkle lightly with powdered sugar.

Jelly or Jam Filling
Hot pepper jelly, marmalades, or any type of jams or jellies may be used. Spread desired amount on omelet before folding.

Enlarge ornaments to make a gift box

Weave ribbons through slits along flat sides of an unassembled gift box

A gaggle of multifolded geese are charming as a table runner, and as matching place cards

OPPOSITE *These girls are making the unusual yarn gift box shown top right on page 108. First, holes are punched down the folded edges of an unassembled box, the box is assembled, and then colorful yarn is woven through the holes and tied on top to create a bow*

Decorating with paper materials

Multifold starburst

A hostess tree covered with gift and candy-filled ornaments

OVERLEAF *Bûche de Noël*

Bûche de Noël

1½ ounces bittersweet cooking chocolate, chopped
2 tablespoons unsalted butter
5 eggs, separated
2 to 3 drops lemon juice
½ cup plus 3 tablespoons granulated sugar
1¼ cups sifted cake flour
Coffee Syrup
Chocolate Mousse
Soft Fudge Icing
½ cup whipping cream, whipped
Meringue Mushrooms
Chocolate curls
Sifted powdered sugar

Combine chocolate and butter in top of double boiler. Heat over simmering water until melted. Cool. Beat egg whites with lemon juice until soft peaks form. Gradually beat in the granulated sugar. Continue beating until stiff but not dry. Lightly beat egg yolks. Fold into egg whites just until blended. Stir a small amount of egg mixture into cooled chocolate. Fold chocolate into remaining egg mixture. Slowly add flour, folding just until blended.

Pour batter into a 17 × 11-inch buttered jelly roll pan lined with buttered parchment paper. Spread batter evenly over pan, smoothing top. Bake at 425 degrees for 9 to 10 minutes. Turn cake out, upside down onto wax paper. Let cool until lukewarm. Carefully peel off parchment paper. Brush cake generously, but evenly, with Coffee Syrup, reserving 2 to 3 tablespoons syrup to brush on while rolling. (Cake must be moist or it will crack while being rolled.) Spread a layer of Chocolate Mousse ⅛-inch thick over cake. Roll up cake from long side, brushing top as needed with reserved syrup. Place cake on a serving platter, seam-side down. Cover and chill for 1 hour.

Cut 1-inch slice off each end of cake at an angle. Place slices on top of cake to resemble knots. Spread Soft Fudge Icing over cake, reserving about ¼ cup for Meringue Mushrooms. For bark effect, lightly score icing lengthwise with fork dipped in warm water. Using a pastry bag, pipe a circle of whipped cream around cut ends of log and around flat top edge of each knot. Spoon about 1 teaspoon reserved fudge icing into center of each ring of whipped cream. Smooth off ends of log and knots. Garnish with Meringue Mushrooms and chocolate curls. Sprinkle powdered sugar lightly over chocolate curls. Chill.

Makes 12 to 16 servings.

Coffee Syrup
¾ cup sugar
½ cup water
⅓ cup strong coffee

Combine sugar, water, and coffee in a saucepan over medium heat. Cook, stirring for 5 minutes. Let cool.

Chocolate Mousse
3 ounces bittersweet cooking chocolate, chopped
3 tablespoons strong coffee
4 egg whites
2 to 3 drops lemon juice
3 tablespoons sugar

Combine chocolate with coffee in top of double boiler over simmering water. Heat until chocolate is melted. Cool. Beat egg whites with lemon juice until soft peaks form. Gradually beat in the sugar. Continue beating until stiff but not dry. Fold a small amount of whites into cooled chocolate mixture, then fold chocolate mixture into remaining egg whites just until blended. Refrigerate until chilled.

Soft Fudge Icing
1 cup whipping cream
½ pound bittersweet cooking chocolate, chopped
3 tablespoons Irish whiskey

Heat whipping cream to a gentle boil in a small saucepan. Stir in chocolate until melted. Stir in whiskey. Cool to room temperature, stirring occasionally, until mixture has a thick fudge consistency.

Meringue Mushrooms
4 egg whites
½ cup granulated sugar
1¼ cups powdered sugar
Cocoa

¼ cup is fine.

Beat egg whites until soft peaks form. Gradually beat in granulated sugar, beating until stiff but not dry. Fold in powdered sugar. Line baking sheet with parchment paper. Using a pastry bag, pipe balls of meringue about the size of a quarter onto paper. For stems, pipe 1½-inch long strips of meringue. Bake at 200 to 250 degrees for about 1 hour or until thoroughly dried. To form mushrooms, gently hollow out underside of caps. Place a dab of reserved icing inside hollow and place pointed end of stem in cap. Sprinkle mushrooms with cocoa.

Coffee Old-Fashioned

1½ teaspoons instant coffee
½ cup cold water
2 teaspoons sugar
2 dashes bitters
¼ cup club soda
3 tablespoons bourbon
Orange slice, maraschino cherry for garnish

Dissolve coffee in cold water. Dissolve sugar and bitters in 2 tablespoons of the club soda. Add bourbon and coffee. Pour over ice cubes in a double old-fashioned glass. Add remaining club soda. Garnish with orange slice and maraschino cherry.

Makes 1 serving.

9
Christmas Day

The weeks of preparations come together on Christmas Day. If you haven't been to *too* many parties, there's time for one final effort and it involves a special brunch for the family and any friends who may drop by.

Center the brunch around the wonderful turkey roll recipe included here that was developed by the U.S. Culinary Olympics team and which won hands down several years ago. It's a lot easier to prepare than you might think. The roll can be made and refrigerated the day before and baked just before serving. Serve it with fresh asparagus (we've included the recipe) as well as some mashed potatoes. If you are not up to such a fancy presentation, make some pancakes Christmas morning in different shapes—there's no doubt that your kids will love them. And have some juice with them, too.

Peanut Batter and Jelly Pancakes

2 cups packaged pancake or buttermilk biscuit mix
1 cup finely chopped peanuts
$\frac{1}{2}$ teaspoon ground cinnamon
2 tablespoons brown sugar
Jelly, jam, or fruit syrups

Prepare pancakes according to package directions. Stir in peanuts, cinnamon, and brown sugar. Allow to stand for 10 minutes before baking. Spoon $\frac{1}{4}$ cup batter onto lightly greased heated griddle for each pancake. Bake until browned on one side, then turn and cook other side. Serve pancakes topped with jelly, jam, or fruit syrup.

Makes about 14 4-inch pancakes.

Banana Nut Pancakes

2 cups packaged pancake or buttermilk biscuit mix
$\frac{1}{2}$ teaspoon ground cinnamon
1 cup chopped walnuts or pecans
3 to 4 small bananas, peeled and sliced
Fruit syrup or honey

Prepare pancakes according to package directions. Add cinnamon and nuts and allow batter to stand for 10 minutes before using. Spoon $\frac{1}{4}$ cup measure onto lightly greased, heated griddle for each pancake. Immediately top with 5 slices banana. When pancake is lightly browned on bottom, turn and cook other side. Serve pancakes with fruit syrup or honey.

Makes about 14 4-inch pancakes.

A Visual Photo Album and a Photo Doll

Keep the memories of the holidays by taking photographs. Rather than adding to the family album (which is admired too infrequently) make a "visual" family photo archive. Whether it's pictures taken on a field trip to the zoo or of your Christmas tree, this project is a clever way to record a memory. Prints of various sizes can be ordered from negatives and can be mounted with spray adhesive to pieces of sugar pine. A coping saw can be used to silhouette the figures. We've also included a photo doll, taken with a Polaroid camera, which you can mount as a tree ornament. Detailed instructions are on page 167.

Blueberry Buttermilk Pancakes

2 cups packaged pancake or buttermilk biscuit mix
Buttermilk
2 teaspoons grated lemon peel
2 tablespoons sugar
Fresh, canned, or frozen blueberries, well drained
Yogurt or sour cream

Prepare pancake batter according to package directions, using buttermilk as the liquid. Stir in lemon peel and sugar. Fold in 1 cup blueberries. Let batter stand for 10 minutes before baking. Spoon ¼ cup batter onto heated, lightly greased griddle for each pancake. Bake until lightly browned on one side, then turn and bake on other side. Serve with a dollop of yogurt or sour cream mixed with additional blueberries.

Makes about 14 4-inch pancakes.

Chocolate Chip Pancakes

2 cups packaged pancake or buttermilk biscuit mix
2 tablespoons brown sugar
½ teaspoon vanilla
½ cup chopped pecans or walnuts
¾ cup semisweet chocolate pieces
Fruit syrup or hot chocolate sauce

Prepare pancake batter according to package directions. Add brown sugar, vanilla, nuts, and chocolate pieces. Mix lightly and allow to stand for 10 minutes before using. Spoon ¼ cup batter onto heated, lightly greased griddle for each pancake. Bake until lightly browned on one side, then flip and cook other side. Serve with fruit syrup or a hot chocolate sauce.

Makes 12 to 14 4-inch pancakes.

Gingerbread Men and Star-Shaped Pancakes

To make these "shaped" pancakes, follow the recipe below.

Pancake Dough

1 egg
1 cup milk
1 14-ounce package gingerbread mix
2 tablespoons butter or margarine, melted
Honey or syrup, flavored with grated orange peel
Gum drops or other candies for decoration

Beat together the eggs and milk. Thoroughly blend in the gingerbread mix and stir in the butter. Place a large gingerbread man cookie cutter mold on a lightly greased griddle. Pour in about 2 tablespoons batter—just enough to barely fill in mold. Brown over low heat; when pancake is firm, remove mold, flip pancake, and brown on the other side. Decorate as desired. Serve with honey.

Makes about 10 gingerbread men pancakes.

For star pancake:

Proceed as above, only using a star-shaped cake mold. Pour batter to just fill in corner of star mold—cake will swell once cooked. Cook at least 3 minutes over medium-low heat until pancake seems firm and bubbles appear on surface; remove mold, turn, and cook for another 2 to 3 minutes. Decorate as desired.

A Polaroid portrait of your child personalizes this Photo Doll

118

The zebra the little girl is sitting on and the one she's holding show a clever way of using two sizes of prints made from the same photo negative

119

A collection of photos mounted on sugar pine become a "living" three-dimensional photo album

121   OVERLEAF *Turkey Breast Oklahoma is served at a festive Christmas brunch*

Turkey Breast Oklahoma

1½ pounds boneless turkey breast, chopped
¼ pound fatback
1 egg
Salt, pepper
5 ounces dark turkey meat, cut julienne style
Stuffing
Butter

Grind turkey breast meat and fatback in a food processor or meat grinder. Blend egg, and salt and pepper to taste into ground meat. Fold in dark meat strips by hand. Place a piece of plastic wrap on counter and pat meat out on it into rectangle approximately ¼-inch thick. Spread a ¼-inch-thick layer of Stuffing over meat. Using plastic wrap to keep meat roll together, roll up jelly roll fashion. Carefully transfer to a roasting pan. Discard plastic wrap. Smooth edges together and pat top with wet hands to round. Bake at 375 degrees for 1 to 1½ hours in roasting pan, basting 4 times with butter and drippings. Allow to stand for 10 minutes before slicing to serve.

Makes 6 servings.

Stuffing
¾ cup chopped onions
2 cloves garlic, minced
¾ cup diced carrots
½ cup chopped parsley
⅓ cup butter or margarine
½ pound mushrooms, diced
3 ounces Virginia ham, diced
3 green onions, sliced
Sage
Thyme
3 ounces turkey liver and giblets, cooked and diced
2 egg yolks
1½ cups coarse bread crumbs
Salt, pepper

Sauté onions, garlic, carrots, and parsley in butter until onions are soft. Add mushrooms, ham, and green onions. Season to taste with sage and thyme. Sauté 2 or 3 minutes longer. Add turkey livers and giblets and cook 2 minutes longer. Remove from heat and stir in egg yolks and bread crumbs. Blend mixture well and season to taste with salt and pepper. Cool before spreading on ground turkey mixture.

Note: Fatback is pork fat. It is available in some supermarkets but is more easily obtained at specialty butcher shops. The Virginia ham usually can be found in delicatessens. If not available, substitute baked ham (preferably one with a Southern cure).

Asparagus with Browned Butter

¼ cup butter
1 tablespoon lemon juice
2½ pounds fresh or frozen asparagus spears
Chopped parsley

Heat butter in a small skillet or saucepan until light brown. Do not burn. Stir in lemon juice. Keep warm. Cook asparagus spears just until tender-crisp. At serving time, pour butter over asparagus and sprinkle with chopped parsley.

Makes 6 to 8 servings.

Diagram 1

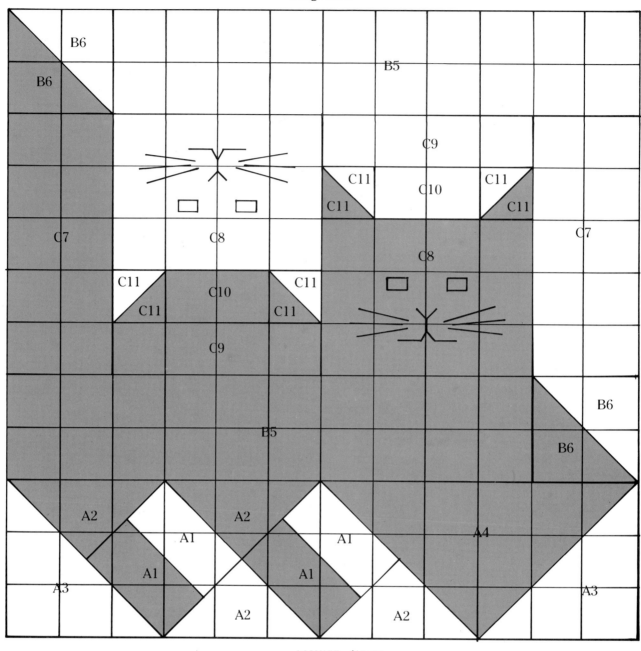

1 SQUARE = ½ INCH
1 QUILT BLOCK = 12 × 12"

For each quilt block, this pattern must be enlarged to 12 inches, either on graph paper or by having a photostat made.

Project Instructions

Chapter 1
CAT QUILT

QUILT INSTRUCTIONS
Finished size of this quilt is 76 inches by 97 inches.

MATERIALS
90 × 180-inch polyester batting
(Note: Yardage is approximate to allow for matching of stripes, and all specifications are for 44-inch-wide fabric.)
6 yards (backing)
4½ yards (dark print)
4½ yards (light print)
3½ yards (middle-value color)
3 yards (border fabric)
½ yard of four different prints (for balls)
Threads
Embroidery thread
Plastic for templates (we used picture-framing plastic)
Graph paper for pattern

TOOLS
Sewing machine
X-Acto knife
No. 11 blade
Charvoz cutting base
Straight pins
Metal straightedge
Embroidery hoop

Selecting fabric:
For strong contrast in the cat patterns, choose a dark fabric and a light fabric for the cat colors. The background fabric should blend with both of those colors and be a middle-value color.

Making the pattern:
Enlarge the pattern (as indicated on Diagram 1) to 12 inches. That can be done by redrawing on graph paper or by having a photostat print made.

Making the templates:
A strong template is needed for cutting many pieces. We used picture-framing plastic cut to the sizes needed. The plastic is first scored with an X-Acto knife, then cracked along a hard edge of a table. Make the templates by tracing the pattern pieces on plastic, adding a ⅜-inch seam allowance on each piece. Some pieces of the pattern are duplicate shapes, so make only one template per shape. Make templates for pattern pieces A-1, A-2, A-3, A-4, B-5, B-6, C-7, C-8, C-9, C-10, C-11.

Cutting pattern pieces:
It is important that all pieces be cut accurately. We used an X-Acto knife with a No. 11 blade and a Charvoz cutting base for cutting all pieces. It took about four hours to cut all the pieces using this method. Next, stack pieces in a flat box; then assemble quilt according to construction procedures.

Sewing the pieces into blocks:
There are 37 blocks to complete the Cat Quilt. Of those, 26 are identical and 11 differ according to their placement on the quilt. To create the cat-leg top borders, you will need to make Rectangle A an additional 7 times. (See Diagram 2.)
1. Sew pieces together to form rectangles A, two Bs, and C.
2. Press seams open.
3. Stitch rectangles together to form blocks.
4. Press blocks.

NUMBER OF FABRIC PIECES NEEDED

template	dark	light	background
A-1	58	63	28
A-2	74	74	28
A-3	74	84	28
A-4	37	37	
B-5	37	37	
B-6	74	74	
C-7	37	37	
C-8	37	37	
C-9	37	37	
C-10	37	37	
C-11	148	148	

Background pieces (no templates)	Border pieces (no templates)
4 2 × 14-inch strips	2 2 × 76-inch strips
3 2 × 12-inch strips	2 2 × 97-inch strips
1 9 × 10-inch strip	
2 6 × 12-inch strips	
2 3 × 72-inch strips	

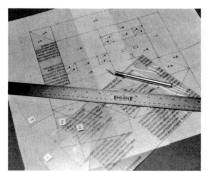
Enlarge the quilt pattern by transferring it to graph paper.

Templates were cut to size from picture-framing plastic.

Stack like pieces together. Pieces were cut with an X-Acto knife.

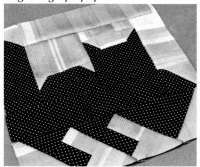
Sew pieces into blocks.

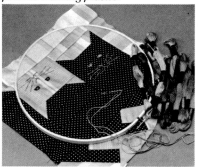
Using an embroidery hoop and colored embroidery thread, hand-stitch a cat face on each block.

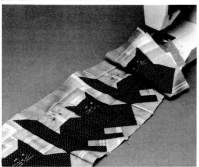
For each long panel, pin right sides of blocks together, tail to tail, then stitch.

Embroidery of cat faces:
Use an embroidery hoop and several colors of embroidery thread. We used a satin stitch for the cats' eyes and a backstitch for the noses, mouths, and whiskers.

Piecing blocks together:
1. To form long panels, pin right sides together, cat's tail to cat's tail. Stitch together (using ³⁄₈-inch seam allowance), adding background pieces according to quilt Diagram 3.
2. Sew cat's legs (Rectangle A) into a panel.
3. Pin right sides of two panels together, lining up tail tips (B-6) with tips of front legs (A-4). Those points should touch. Follow quilt pattern for placement of panels.
4. Stitch long 3 × 72-inch background panels to top and bottom of quilt.

Adding borders:
Pin and stitch border strips to quilt with right sides together, mitering corners.

Finishing the quilt:
1. Measure finished size of pieced top.
2. Prepare the backing by sewing yardage together to approximate dimensions of pieced top. Cut off excess fabric to match exact dimensions of pieced top.
3. Lay batting on a large, flat surface.
4. Place the pieced top directly on

top, right side up.
5. Place the backing on top of the pieced top, right sides together.
6. Make sure all layers of fabrics are smooth and even. Pin corners. Stretch and pin the layers together.
7. Stitch all four edges, leaving a 24-inch opening on one side for turning. Trim corners and turn quilt inside out.

Machine quilting:
1. Baste all layers together.
2. Machine-quilt around the outer edges of all dark cats. Begin at the center and work outward, rolling half of quilt under the arm of the machine. Check backing often to avoid puckering. Adjust machine tension if necessary.
3. Stitch around borders.

Making and appliquéing balls (41 are required):
1. For each ball of each color, piece four 2 × 2-inch squares of fabric together, using a ¹⁄₄-inch seam, to form a 3 ¹⁄₂-inch-square block.
2. Place two blocks of the same color with right sides together. Draw a 3-inch circle on fabric and stitch circle (using a ¹⁄₄-inch seam), leaving ³⁄₄-inch opening for turning. Trim corners and turn.
3. Stuff balls with excess quilt batting.
4. Whipstitch to close balls, and appliqué balls onto quilt after machine

quilting is completed.

Cat Pillow:
1. Piece together one cat block, same as for quilt.
2. Add one Rectangle A to make the legs of the inverted cat (i.e. striped cat of our pattern).
3. Add a 2-inch print border on all sides.
4. Add a 2-inch solid border around the print border.
5. Make a 1-inch strip of self-piping and stitch or pin around outer edges.
6. Follow basic directions above for finishing the quilt (allowing for size differences and leaving only a 6-inch opening for turning) and making and appliquéing the ball.

Diagram 2

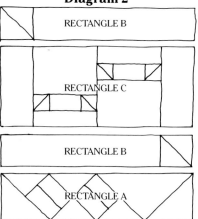

RECTANGLE B

RECTANGLE C

RECTANGLE B

RECTANGLE A

Diagram 3

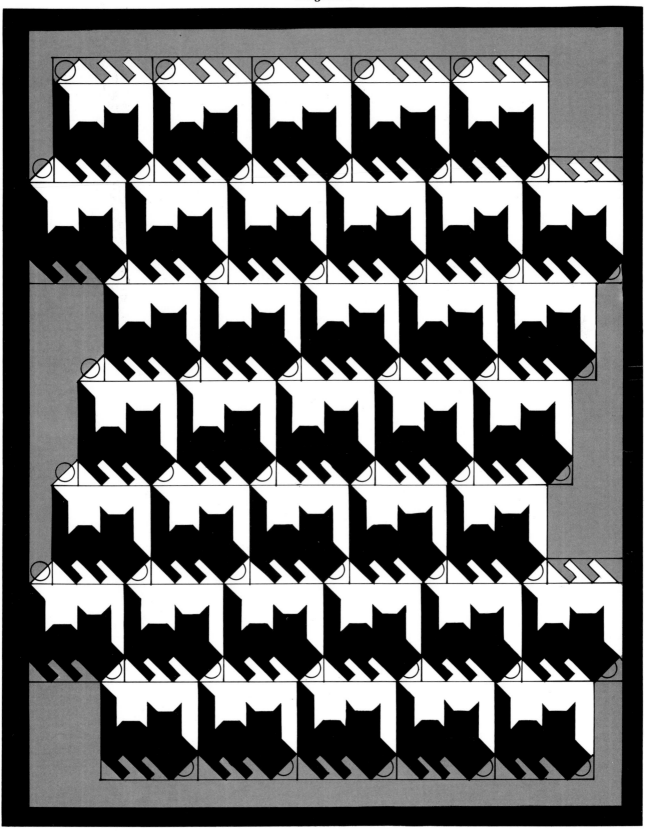

Quilt blocks should be pieced together according to the diagram above

TEDDY BEAR

Here are brief guidelines for making a sitting 12-inch teddy bear.

MATERIALS
Bond paper
Pencil, chalk, scissors
Fabric for bear
Fabric for collar
Straight pins
Polyester fiberfill
Buttons for eyes
Buttons for joints
Upholstery needle, nylon cord

1. Trace pattern on fabric. Cut through both layers of fabric; give ¼-inch seam allowance. Pin bodywrap pattern to single strip of fabric, wrong side up. Cut.
2. Pin fabric parts together with right sides together, adjusting fit as needed. Baste if necessary. Machine stitch as follows: Start at nose tip and attach bodywrap completely around one body profile, ending at underside of chin. Leave opening here to allow for stuffing. Stitch on second profile, stopping at same point under chin. Turn right side out and stuff with fiberfill for desired plumpness. Slip-stitch to close openings.
3. Assemble and stitch arm and leg pieces (including paw pads) with right sides together, leaving a 2½-inch opening. Turn right side out, stuff, and slip-stitch to close. Sew ear pieces in same manner and hand-stitch to bear head. Sew eyes to face. Cover joint buttons with fabric.
4. To attach arms to body: Thread nylon cord through upholstery needle. Push needle into shoulder and through body, leaving cord dangling at entry. Slip one joint button onto thread, push needle back through body, add second button. Tie off in armpit. Test for snug fit. Repeat for legs.
5. Finally, create ruffled collar from two strips of fabric scraps, 4 inches wide by 36 inches long. With right sides together, make ¼-inch seams on both long sides. Turn right side out and string a cord through the casing (curtain style). Adjust gathers until perfect, and tie at back of teddy's neck. Fold in raw edges, slip-stitch ends together.

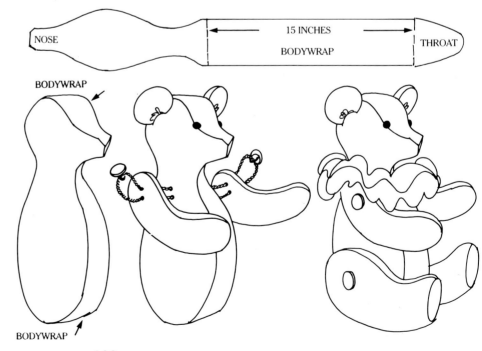

NOSE   15 INCHES   THROAT
            BODYWRAP

BODYWRAP

BODYWRAP

BEAR BODY PROFILE *(cut 2)*

THROAT

THROAT

NOSE

EARS *(cut 4)*

131

ARM

NOSE

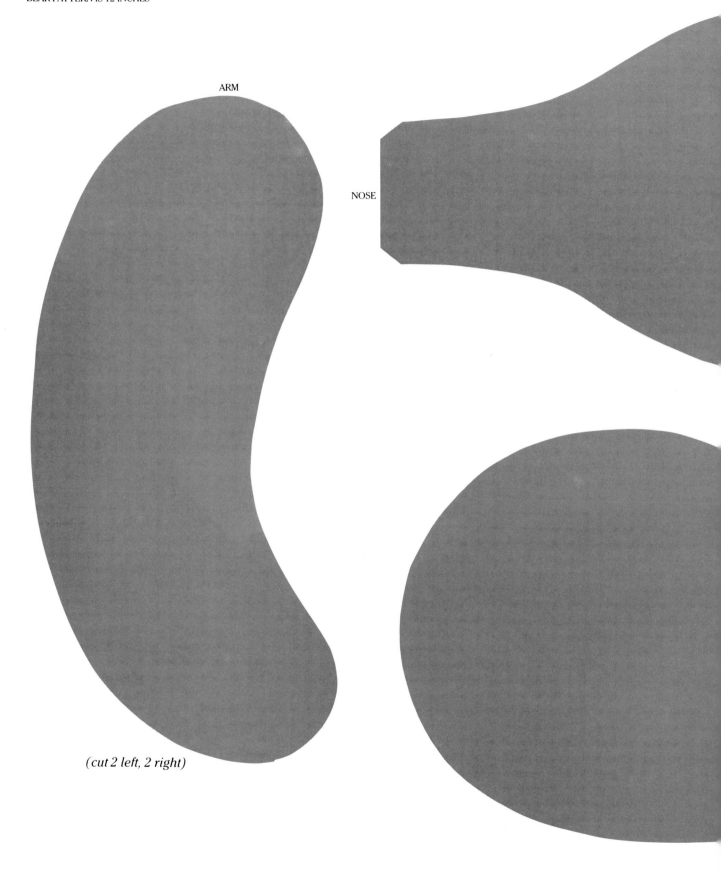

(cut 2 left, 2 right)

BODYWRAP *(cut 1)*

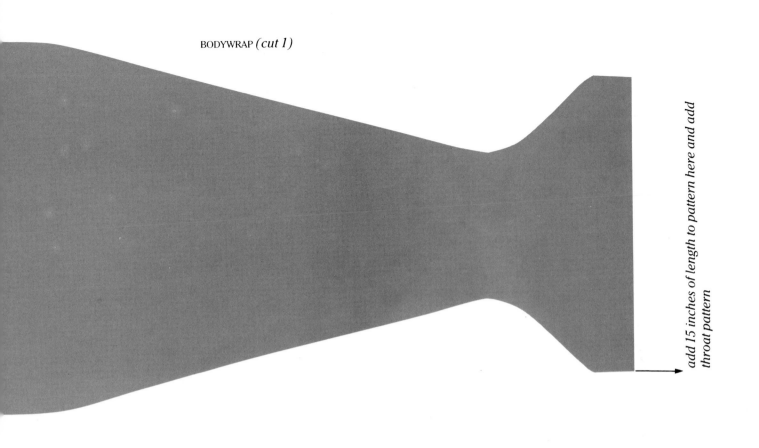

add 15 inches of length to pattern here and add throat pattern

PAW PAD *(cut 2)*

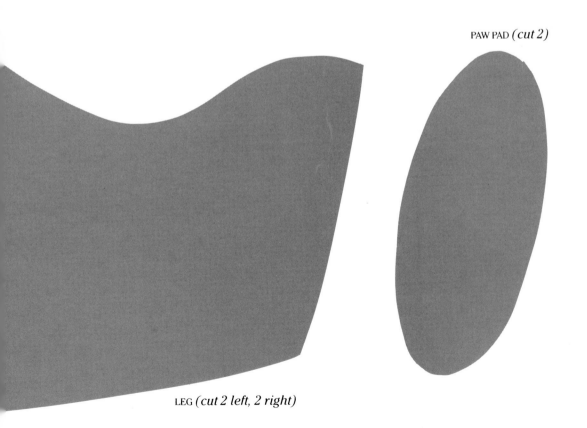

LEG *(cut 2 left, 2 right)*

133

COUNTRY DOLLS

The following instructions are for making a small doll with a wooden head 2 inches in diameter. The body is about 5 inches long; the legs are 6 inches long; the arms consist of 2 inches of fabric and 2 inches of wood spindle. (The pattern can be traced as is, or enlarged to make a doll of any size.) Different types of fabric will change the final shape of the doll; heavier fabrics need firmer stuffing for more fullness in the arms and legs. The length of the legs can be adjusted according to the length of the dress. Because the drawstrings that tighten the fabric arms around the wooden arms will show, the cord or yarn you select should be coordinated with the dress fabric.

MATERIALS FOR ONE DOLL

Graph paper or photostat enlargement
    of body pattern and dress pattern
Pencil
Scissors
Small fret saw
About ⅓ yard 36-inch-wide stretch
    polyester fabric
About ⅓ yard 36-inch-wide print fabric
Straight pins
Thread
About 1⅓ yards narrow cord or yarn
    for drawstrings
Polyester fiberfill
Wood spindles for arms, cut to size
Wood-turning ball for head
Ribbon and lace, optional
Accessories: wig, hat, shoes, socks
Acrylic paints

1. To begin with, transfer each pattern onto graph paper, adding ⅜-inch seam allowance on all edges, or else have a photostat enlargement made to the exact size.
2. Pin body pattern to stretch polyester fabric and cut out body sections. You'll need two body pieces, four arm pieces, and four leg pieces.
3. To make arms: Place yarn (about

six inches) at bottom edge of fabric, turn seam allowance over yarn and stitch casing, leaving ends open. With right sides together, stitch side seams. Turn right side out.
4. To make legs: With right sides together, stitch leg seams. Leave top open for stuffing. Turn and stuff.
5. To make body: First, stitch darts in back of body fabric. Make drawstring casing at shoulder and neck openings same as for arms. With right sides together, pin arms onto body fabric from the inside. Stitch side seams, incorporating arms. Leave bottom edge open. Insert legs into bottom of body with right sides together and toes facing forward. Stitch body and legs together. Turn body right side out and stuff.
6. Insert head, pull up drawstring, and tie securely.
7. Stuff arms. Insert wood spindles, pull up drawstrings, and tie securely.
8. To make dress: Pin dress pattern to print fabric and cut. Make drawstring

Body Pattern

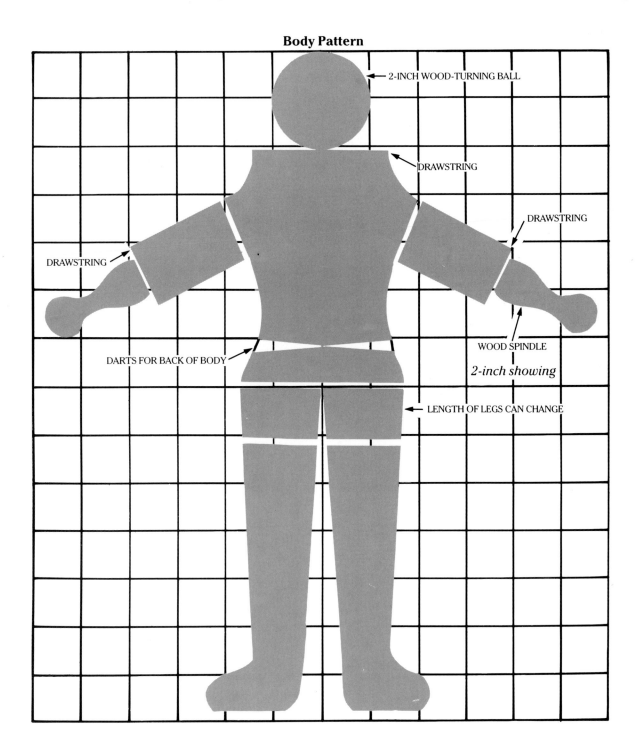

←— 2-INCH WOOD-TURNING BALL

DRAWSTRING

DRAWSTRING

DRAWSTRING

WOOD SPINDLE

2-inch showing

DARTS FOR BACK OF BODY

←— LENGTH OF LEGS CAN CHANGE

casings at neck and arm openings same as for arms and neck of body. Stitch side seams. Turn dress right side out. Hem to desired length.

9. Paint face with acrylic paints. To complete the project, add wig, hat, shoes, and any additional accessories desired (available at many doll and hobby shops).

Dress Pattern

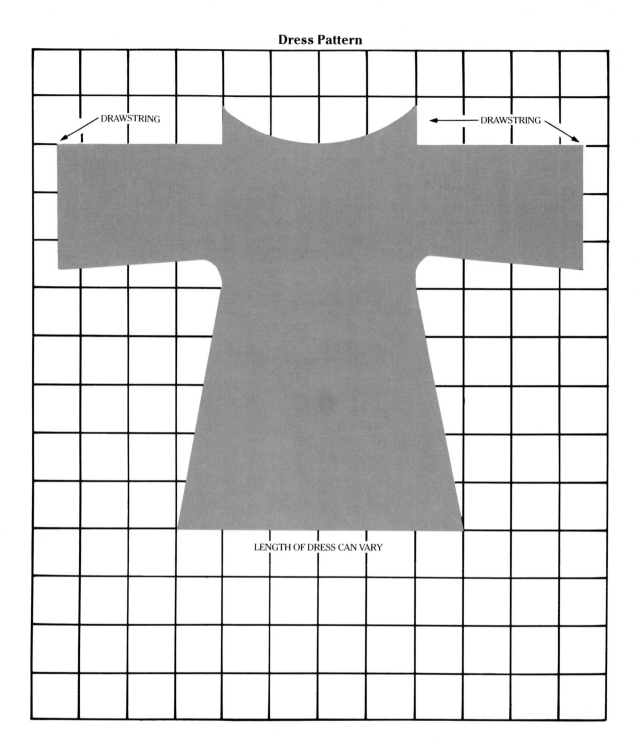

DRAWSTRING

DRAWSTRING

LENGTH OF DRESS CAN VARY

WOOD-TURNING TOYS

Wood turnings come in a variety of sizes, lengths, and shapes. It might be difficult to match the sizes shown in the diagrams pictured here. so use them as a guide for creating your own wood turnings. Below are specific instructions for the tower construction; use the same method for making the wood figure, Jack's box, and the horse.

TOWER SIZE: 36 inches tall

MATERIALS
Precut wood components
¼-inch dowel cut in 1-inch lengths
½-inch dowel cut in 1½-inch lengths
1-inch clear pine, cut to sizes needed
Spray paints and primer
Sandpaper
Pencil

TOOL
Drill with ¼- and ½-inch bits

TOWER CONSTRUCTION
1. Arrange wood components to form toy design.
2. With a pencil, mark the points where dowels will be inserted.
3. Drill holes for dowels.
4. Insert dowels and assemble.
5. Disassemble to paint. Sand and paint each piece individually. For a high-gloss finish, use a primer spray with two coats of paint.
6. Reassemble.

Wood Figure: 19 inches tall
Follow instructions for tower.

3¼" DIAMETER × 4½"
HIGH CAP POST (HEAD)

½" DOWEL

1¼ × 5" GRILL SPINDLE (ARM)

3½ × 7" GRILL SPINDLE (BODY)

¼" DOWEL

1½" DIAMETER KNOB (HAND)

¼" DOWEL

1½ × 7½" GRILL SPINDLE (LEG)

1½" DIAMETER KNOB (FOOT)

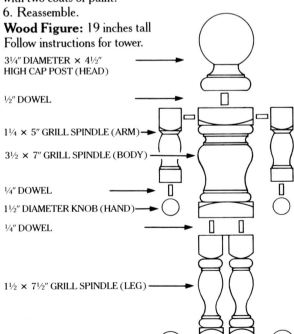

Tower

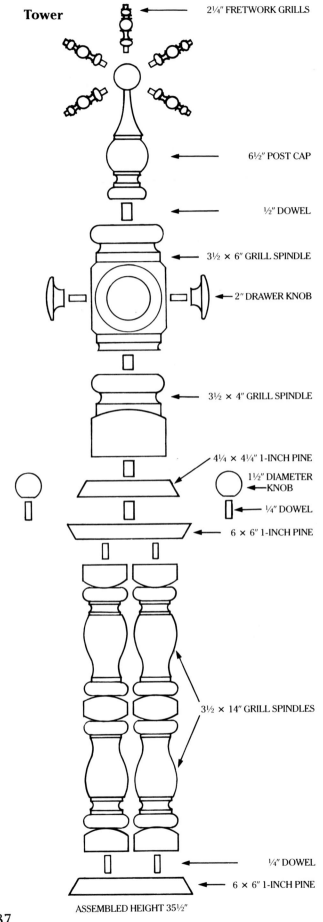

2¼" FRETWORK GRILLS

6½" POST CAP

½" DOWEL

3½ × 6" GRILL SPINDLE

2" DRAWER KNOB

3½ × 4" GRILL SPINDLE

4¼ × 4¼" 1-INCH PINE

1½" DIAMETER KNOB

¼" DOWEL

6 × 6" 1-INCH PINE

3½ × 14" GRILL SPINDLES

¼" DOWEL

6 × 6" 1-INCH PINE

ASSEMBLED HEIGHT 35½"

137

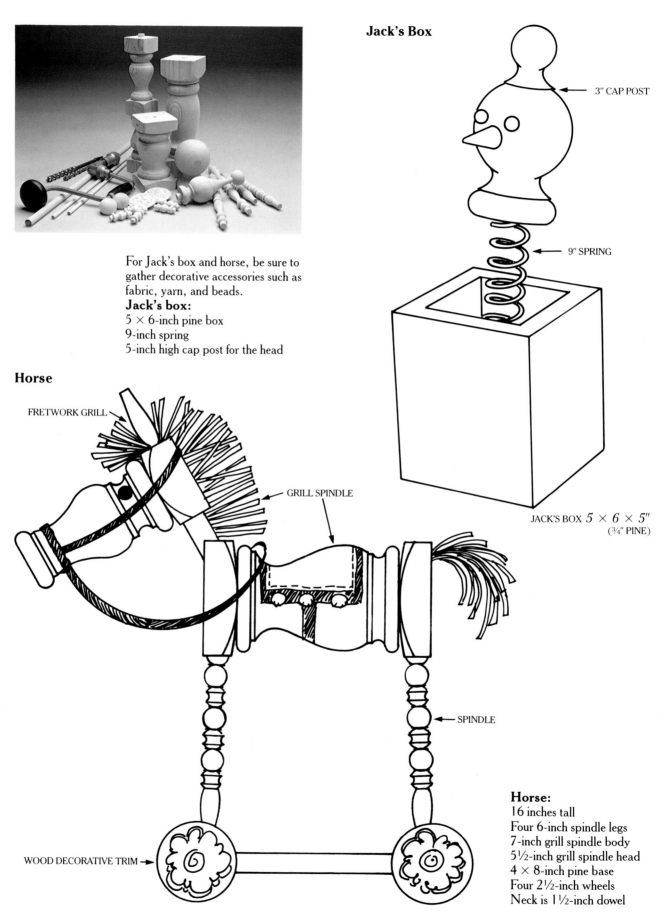

Jack's Box

3" CAP POST

9" SPRING

For Jack's box and horse, be sure to gather decorative accessories such as fabric, yarn, and beads.

Jack's box:
5 × 6-inch pine box
9-inch spring
5-inch high cap post for the head

JACK'S BOX 5 × 6 × 5"
(¾" PINE)

Horse

FRETWORK GRILL

GRILL SPINDLE

SPINDLE

WOOD DECORATIVE TRIM

Horse:
16 inches tall
Four 6-inch spindle legs
7-inch grill spindle body
5½-inch grill spindle head
4 × 8-inch pine base
Four 2½-inch wheels
Neck is 1½-inch dowel

138

Chapter 2
HAND-PAINTED TABLECLOTH

TABLECLOTH INSTRUCTIONS

The finished tablecloth is 70 inches in diameter. All cotton, it is colored with Tincoton dyes.

MATERIALS

Four 45-inch-square pieces of 100% cotton fabric
Selection of Tincoton dyes
Clear gutta
Paper
Pencil and felt pen

TOOLS

Wood frame for stretching fabric
Two plastic squeeze bottles for gutta
Assortment of brushes

Making the pattern:

To make the 70-inch-diameter table-cloth, you will need this pattern which shows one quarter of the completed design. Enlarge the pattern to 35 inches by transferring it to scale on graph paper or by having a photostat enlargement made to size. Make sure the lines are dark and easy to see.

Preparing your fabric for painting:

Next, stretch your fabric taut over a wooden frame and set it on a flat surface. Place the pattern underneath the frame and trace the design onto the fabric with a graphite pencil. After the design is transferred onto the fabric, retrace over the lines with the gutta, making sure all lines connect; the gutta takes about ten minutes to dry.

139

Tablecloth Pattern

ENLARGE PATTERN TO 35 INCHES (SHOWS ¼ OF ACTUAL DESIGN)

Painting your fabric:
The fabric is now ready to paint with a variety of fabric dyes. The color is applied in the center of the surface area to be painted and spreads out on its own to the edges of the design. After the painting is completed, the fabric is allowed to dry in a horizontal position.

Sewing your fabric together:
Cut the 45-inch-square pieces into triangles. Next, stitch together the four fabric sections. Hem with a zigzag stitch. Matching napkins, using different design segments of the tablecloth art, were fashioned from four 18-inch-square pieces of cotton.

ENLARGE PATTERN TO 12 INCHES—REPEAT 4 TIMES

For the scarf:
1 ½ yards 100% silk
Selection of silk dyes
The instructions for making the silk
scarf are the same, except you will
need silk fabric and dyes for silk instead of cotton fabric and the Tincoton
dyes. Enlarge the scarf pattern to
twelve inches. You will need to repeat
the pattern four times, with two of the
images reversed, on one piece of fabric.

PINE NEEDLE BASKETS

Two basic techniques are described on these pages. Before embarking on either type of basket, remember to dampen brittle materials. They'll be softer, more pliable for fingers unaccustomed to manipulating rough-surface fibers.

MATERIALS

100 pine needle clusters—these may be found under pine trees in private gardens. They may not be removed from Torrey pines or public parks.

Raffia or sea grass of 24-inch lengths. These are used as "weft."

Scissors for cutting and trimming weft and thinning pine needles.

Straight upholstery needle, large eye.

Bowl of water for keeping materials damp and ready to coil.

Coiling:

1. Pine needles should be washed and left to soak. Meanwhile, thread upholstery needle with 24-inch strand of raffia. Then select a single sheaf of pine, damp and pliable.

2. Wrap raffia around bound end of a single pine sheaf, as shown. Secure tightly. With scissors, trim off hard end of sheaf. This makes coiling easier, gives more refinement to the basket. Wrap only one pine sheaf in this fashion.

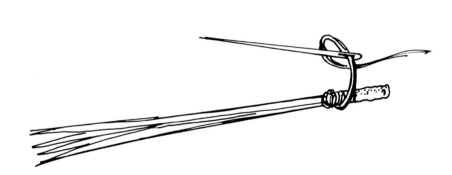

3. Begin coiling this pine sheaf as shown, hold position by securing with raffia and needle. Tighten raffia. Proceed with coiling and securing, attaching additional sheaves about an inch before reaching the tips of the pine needles.

4. Select three pine sheaves. Cluster together, and secure in same manner with needle and raffia. These triple clusters add character to the basket. Continue to coil, secure, and add sheaves until a 3-inch-diameter base has been formed. (To add more raffia, don't knot; sew end into the basket. Add new length and stitch twice to secure.)

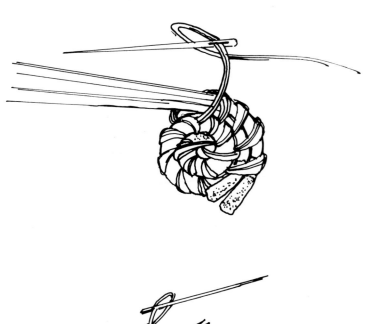

5. Begin to shape the coils as you build the sides of the basket. Layers may gradually be expanded in circumference to create a wider opening, or diminished to form a smaller mouth. Later you'll want to vary the coils for even more surface interest.

To bind off the top layer, thin pine needles with scissors until they almost diminish entirely beneath the final raffia stitches. Weave raffia ends into the coils. If you wish to further embellish, add dried flowers.

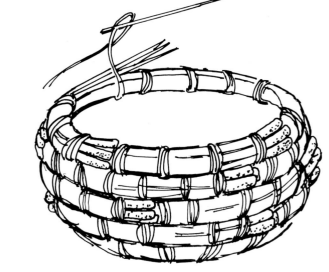

Split-Stitch Variation:

1. More accomplished basket makers enjoy the look of a decorative split stitch. It is introduced only after the central coil on the pine needle basket has been completed. Then add a cluster of three pine sheaves and secure by stitching through a previous stitch.

2. On second round of coiling, be sure to stitch only through previous stitches. This creates the spiral effect shown at right; a pretty, precise finesse.

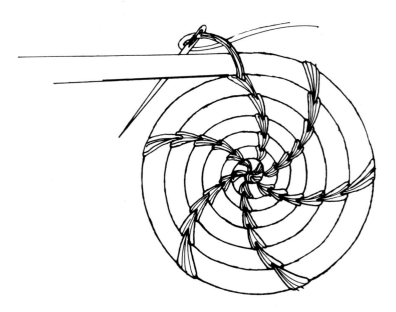

143

Old English Lettering Example

Multiline dip pens, which must be returned periodically to the inkwell, produce from one to five graceful parallel lines. Brass-tipped chisel-point fountain pens spread ink in hairline to 1½-inch widths. Both of these kinds of pens produce some of the finest calligraphy. Children, however, will do best with the new chisel-tip felt markers available.

Start with a chisel-tip fountain pen and the script lettering example provided on page 145. First build a little confidence using the pen with your own handwriting; then look into the variety of tools and books for all sizes and types of lettering.

144

ABCDEFGHIJ
KLMNOPQ
RSTUVWXYZ

abcdefghijklmn
opqrstuvwxyz

Script Lettering Examples

145

RUBBER STAMPS

MATERIALS
Soft lead pencil
Paper
Rubber or plastic erasers
A selection of ink pads
X-Acto knife with a No. 11 blade

1. Using a soft lead pencil, trace pattern on a piece of paper. Fill in all details. Place this drawing on a clear eraser, face down. Press. The drawing will transfer to the eraser.
2. Next, with an X-Acto knife fitted with a No. 11 blade, cut away the eraser at all uncolored areas. (Try to keep clean edges.) Where you've cut away the eraser's surface, there will be no contact with the inked pad. The raised or remaining surface will create the decorative symbols for your stamped-out themes.
3. Buy several different stamp pads and ink colors for each motif, then mix and mingle designs as shown here.

Full-scale Patterns for Steel-engraved Rubber Stamps

Hand-carved Eraser Stamp Patterns

STAMPS ARE FULL SCALE

The 4 Stages of Making a Hand-carved Rubber Stamp

SNOWFLAKE STICKERS

Stickers can be made from any material with an adhesive backing. The stickers portrayed here were made with a material called diffraction grating, which is available in a variety of colors. Papers designed for lining shelves or cabinets, and covering walls can also be used. Use an X-Acto knife with a No. 11 blade and a pair of scissors for cutting.

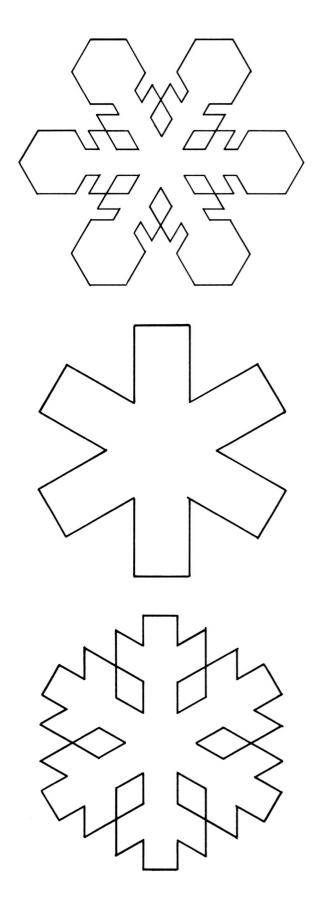

STICKERS ARE FULL SCALE

148

Chapter 4
ACETATE SPICE BOX

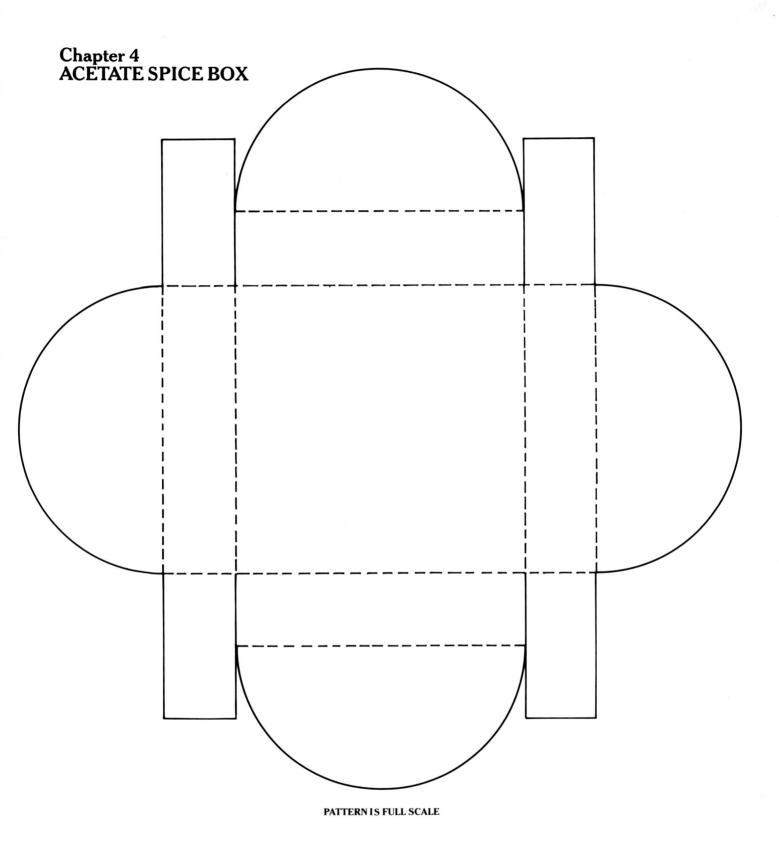

PATTERN IS FULL SCALE

1. Place an 8-inch-by-8-inch sheet of .005 acetate on top of the enlarged pattern. Tape to hold in place. Using an artist's X-Acto knife with a No. 11 blade, lightly cut the acetate on the solid lines of the pattern, being careful not to cut through the lines.
2. With a dull-edged tool, crease the acetate along the dotted lines. Remove tape. Gently tear acetate away from cut edges. Gently fold acetate on creased lines. Fold into a box shape. Tape, or tie with a ribbon to hold the box in shape.

Chapter 5
HORSE AND ANGEL
STICK TOYS

MATERIALS (For 1 toy)
1-inch wooden ball (you will need 2
  balls for the doll)
⅜-inch dowel cut to 10 inches in length
Craft glue
Spray paint—red and white
Selection of felt, lace, ribbon, yarn,
  sequins, pipe cleaners
Polyester filler for stuffing

The horse and angel stick toys can be
  crafted from these patterns.

To make the pattern:
Trace the pattern on heavy paper. Let
the children choose their favorite felt.
Pin the pattern to the cloth and cut out
the figure.

To assemble the horse:
Fold the cloth and glue the edges
together, leaving the bottom open to
insert the dowel and stuffing.

fold of fabric

cut two layers of fabric—folded

150

To assemble the angel:
Secure the two pieces of felt together
and glue edges, leaving space at the
top for the head and insertion of the
dowel. Leave the bottom open to stuff
wings with polyester filler.

To finish the stick toy:
Glue the wood balls to the dowel.
Finish the basic form by inserting the
wooden stick. Using the photographs
on page 71 as guides, trim wings,
halos, and hair for the angels, manes
and reins for the horse.

cut two pieces of fabric

STUFFED CAT TOY

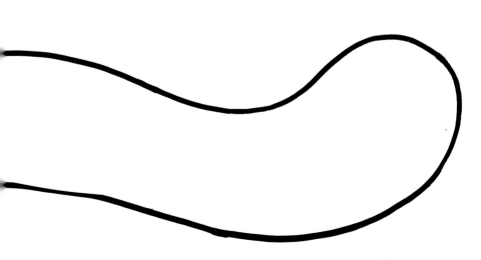

Trace the pattern onto heavy paper.
Cut out. Let each child choose his or
her favorite fabrics. Place two pieces
of fabric face to face. Then pin the
pattern to the cloth. Trace outline of
cat to be used as a sewing line for the
young seamstress. Cut out fabric, allowing ½-inch seam allowance all the way
around cat. Do not cut between legs.
Sew fabric pieces together, leaving an
open space at bottom of cat. Cut once,
between the cat legs. Turn right side
out. Stuff with polyester filler. Close
opening with a whip stitch. Sew eyes
and whiskers in place. Add yarn or
ribbon collar.

COOKIES THAT WALK AWAY

To make the boy, girl, and cat ginger-bread cookies, you will first need to prepare the cookie dough recipe at right. This dough is also for making the gingerbread goose in the "Bake and Give" chapter; however, you won't need to make the base. Decorate these cookie cutouts as desired. The instructions for assembly are part of the recipe.

CAT IS FULL SCALE   **Cat**

Gingerbread Cookie Dough

1½ cups whipping cream
2½ cups brown sugar, packed
1¼ cups dark corn syrup
1 tablespoon ginger
1 tablespoon grated lemon peel
2 tablespoons baking soda
9 cups flour
Icing
Candied fruits, gum drops, etc. for decoration

Mix whipping cream, brown sugar, syrup, ginger, lemon peel, and baking soda together and stir for 10 minutes. Add the flour and work until smooth. Cover and leave in cool place overnight.

Enlarge boy and girl to 11 inches; goose to 8 inches. Cat and base do not need to be enlarged. Transfer patterns to a heavy bond paper. Cut out patterns.

Roll out the dough to ¼-inch thickness and place on a greased baking sheet. Dust patterns with flour, lay patterns over dough, and cut around each one using a sharp knife. Remove extra dough. Lift off patterns, brush cookies with water, and bake on greased baking sheet at 250 degrees for 15 minutes, or until edges are dark brown. (This is one time when *over*baking is necessary.) Leave on baking sheet to cool.

Icing
1 lb. powdered sugar
3 egg whites
½ teaspoon cream of tartar
Food colorings

Beat powdered sugar, cream of tartar, and egg whites together until smooth.

Finishing the cookie: When the cookies have cooled completely, decorate with icing colored with a few drops food coloring of your choice. Use a pastry tube fitted with a small metal tip to draw the faces, hair, clothes, and cat bow.

Glue candied fruits, gum drops, etc. and let dry. Attach cookies to the base using the white icing as a glue.

Cookies will need to be propped upright (such as with coffee mug handles) until icing has dried.

Goose

ENLARGE GOOSE TO 8 INCHES

Base

BASE IS FULL SCALE

For boy and girl patterns, turn the page.
Makes enough for 6 large figures and 3 cats.

155

Base

Girl

ENLARGE BOY AND GIRL TO 11 INCHES

Base

Boy

Chapter 6
CONSTRUCTION OF NOAH'S ARK

MATERIALS
Paper
Pencil
Dremel 15-inch scroll saw
Dremel table saw
Safety goggles
Sandpaper
3 to 4 sheets ³/₁₆-inch aircraft plywood
Spray paints
Spray primer
4 1½-inch lengths of ¼-inch dowel
4 2-inch wood wheels

Using a Dremel scroll saw will result in accurate cuts if you gently follow a pencil line. Learn to draw with the saw, making gentle curves rather than sharp corners.
1. Enlarge drawings 200%. For accuracy, you may choose to have a 200% photostat enlargement made.
2. Enlarge plans as indicated on ark models. Cut out the paper plans for the ark and check for size and fit. Do the same for the animal drawings.

3. Transfer the ark plans onto the plywood.
4. Transfer the animal drawings onto the plywood.
5. Cut straight edges on table saw. (Note: It is very important to cut pieces for a tight fit. It is better to have a slot too small or a tab too large. Pieces can be sanded for a perfect fit.)
6. Cut curves, slots, and holes with scroll saw. When cutting out the animal shapes, draw with the saw blade as you cut. Don't worry about cutting exactly on the line; instead, concentrate on making the cuts smooth and graceful.
7. Check for tight fit.
8. Assemble the basic barn. Fit the inside floor together with the side walls. Add the front and back walls. Add the roof. Add the outside deck. Assemble the boat. Attach the four wheels between the water and the sides of the boat with the dowel. Fit the front and back panels of boat into the side slots and through the water slots. Attach

the bow pieces. Place the barn section into the boat.
9. Disassemble.
10. Finish the wood. Gently sand. Spray with wood sealer or primer and coat with spray paint. We cut stencils for the animal details and patterns but they can be hand-painted, too. If desired, small wheels can be attached to the animals.

PATTERNS SHOULD DOUBLE IN SIZE

³⁄₁₆″ DEEP SLOT.

BASE

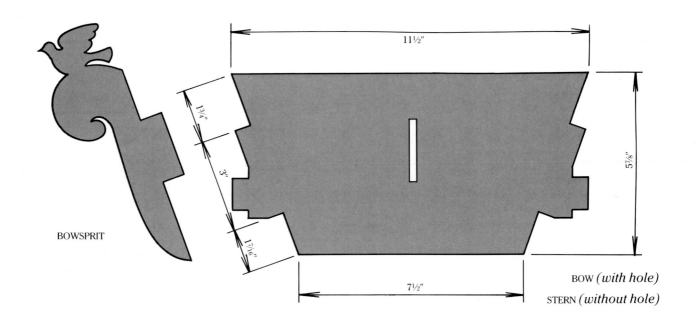

BOWSPRIT

11½"

1¾"

3"

1⁷⁄₁₆"

5⅞"

7½"

BOW *(with hole)*
STERN *(without hole)*

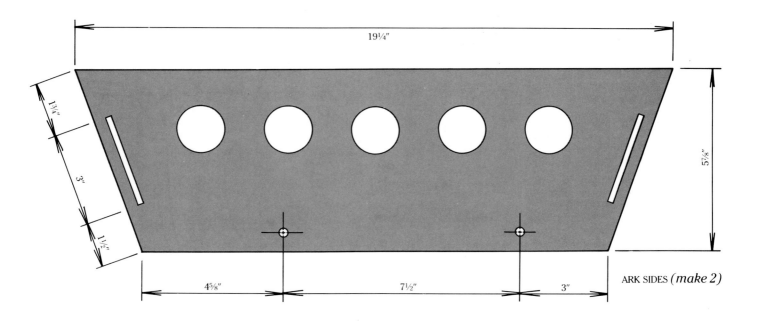

19¼"

1¾"

3"

1½"

5⅞"

4⅝"

7½"

3"

ARK SIDES *(make 2)*

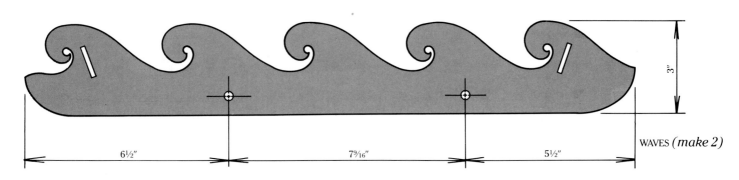

3"

6½"

7⁹⁄₁₆"

5½"

WAVES *(make 2)*

161

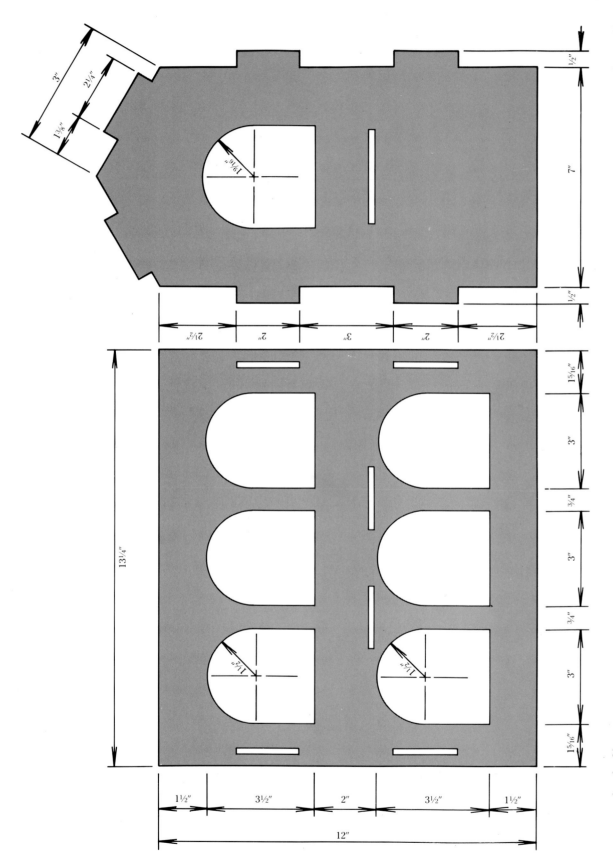

3"
2¼"
1⅜"

1½"

7"

1⁹⁄₁₆"

½"

2½" 2" 3" 2" 2½"

13¼"

1⁵⁄₁₆"
3"
¾"
3"
¾"
3"
1⁵⁄₁₆"

1½"

1½" 3½" 2" 3½" 1½"

12"

BARN SIDES (*make 2*)

162

ROOF *(make 2)*

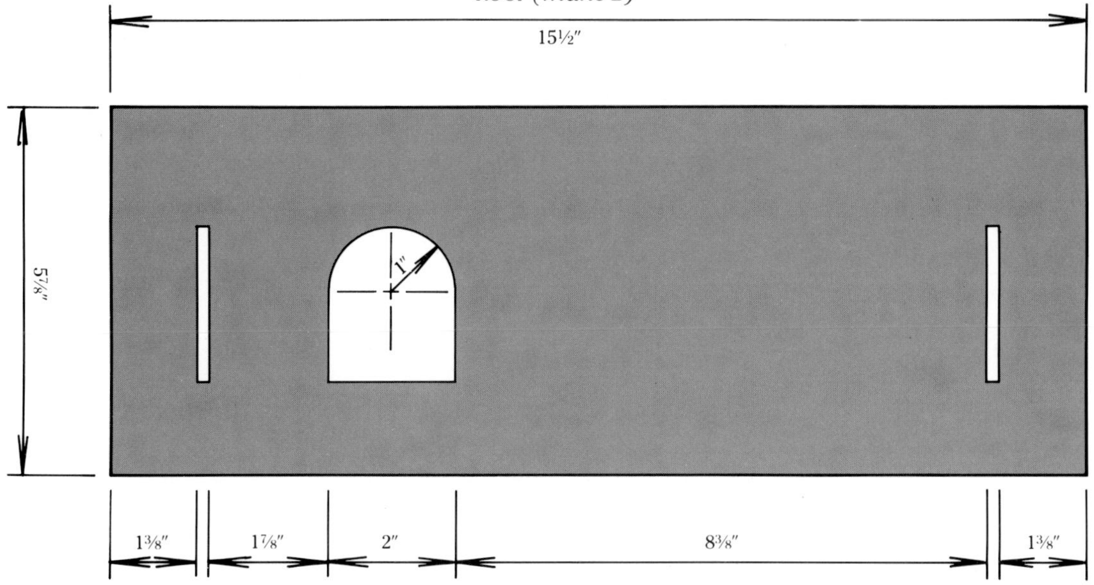
15½″
5⅞″
1″
1⅜″
1⅞″
2″
8⅜″
1⅜″

SECOND FLOOR

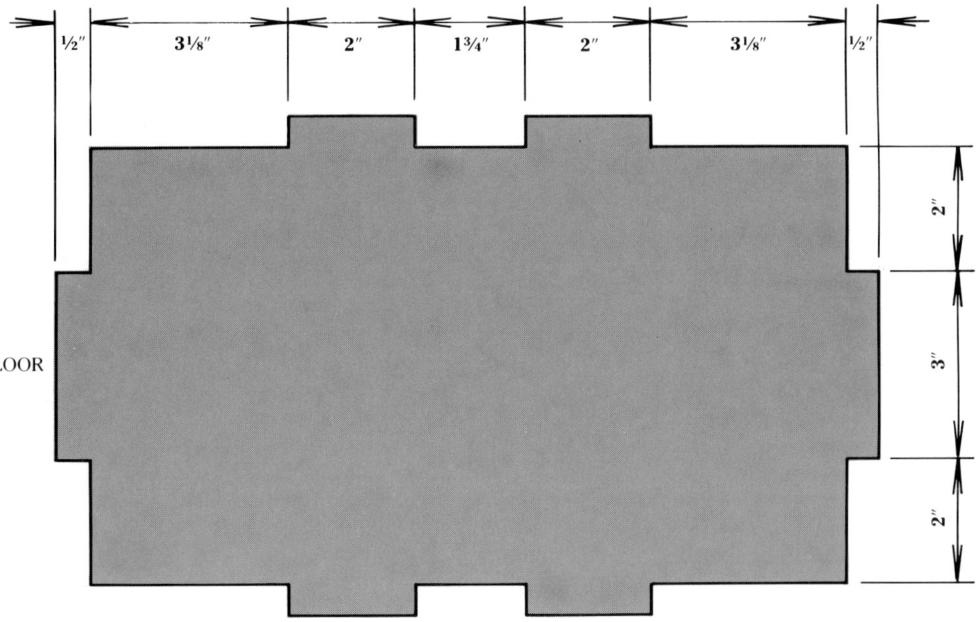
½″
3⅛″
2″
1¾″
2″
3⅛″
½″
2″
3″
2″

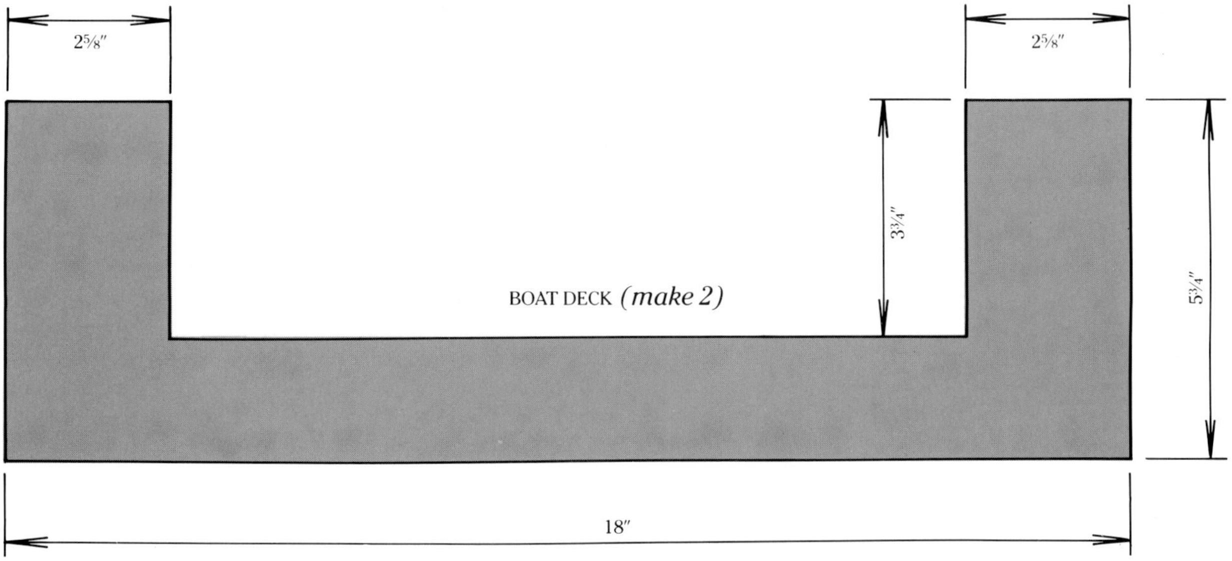
2⅝″
2⅝″
3¾″
BOAT DECK *(make 2)*
5¾″
18″

Chapter 8
ORNAMENTS FOR THE HOUSE AND TREE

MATERIALS

Colored papers
Scissors
X-Acto knife with No. 11 blade
Manicure-type scissors
Straightedge or T-square
Spray adhesive
Glue
Stapler
Grommets
Hole puncher
Ornament hooks
Ribbons and yarn

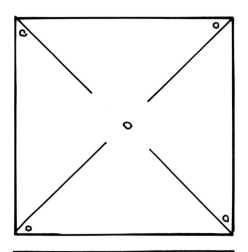

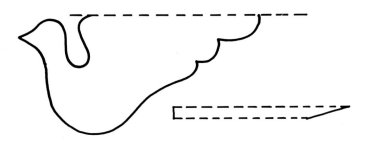

Making a bird:
Fold a 4-inch-square piece of paper in half. Cut out bird shape with wings along fold as shown. To make the tail, accordion-fold a 3-inch-square piece of paper nine times. Cut the tail angle as shown. Glue the tail in place.

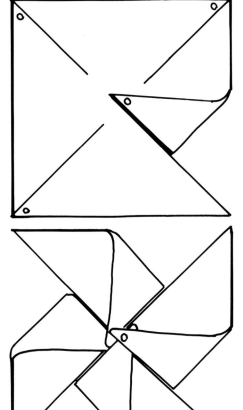

Making a star:
Accordion-fold a 3 × 16-inch strip of paper 31 times. Cut the top angle as shown above. Next, cut half of a star shape, making sure to cut through all the folds. With a hole punch, make a hole at the end of the folded paper as shown and tie a piece of colored string or yarn through. Open the folded paper and then glue the outside edges together.

Making a pinwheel:
Start with a 4-inch-square piece of paper. From each corner, draw a diagonal line to the center of the paper. Punch holes at alternating points and in the center as shown. Cut along each line, taking care not to cut all the way to the center. Fold point ends with holes inward toward center; set with a grommet.

164

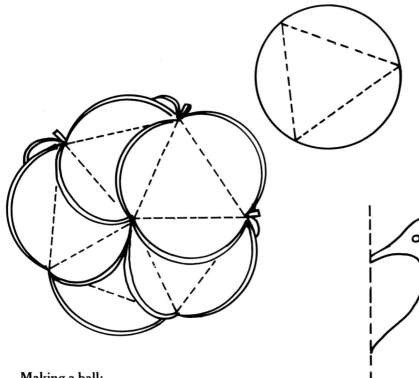

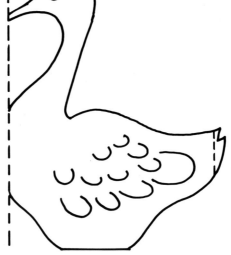

Making a ball:

Cut 20 paper circles in desired size. Score three sides of each circle as shown. Fold sides of circle toward center along score lines to make a triangle (you will have three "petals" per circle as shown). Petal by petal, glue circles together to make a ball. To use as an ornament, punch a hole in one petal and set with a grommet, or thread ribbon through. To use as a container, do not glue down the 20th circle; that circle will become the lid.

Making a goose:

Fold the desired size of two-ply Strathmore paper in half. Draw a goose, making sure the beak and chest are at the folded edge as shown. Cut out. Cut out eye and feathers and fold feathers upward for three-dimensional effect. To make package decoration, accordion-fold desired length of paper, then follow above instructions. Glue or tape end geese together.

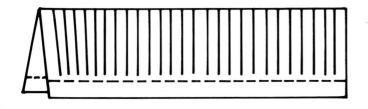

Making a sunburst:

Fold a 2 × 4-inch piece of paper in half. Score along the length of the outside edges, as shown by dotted line. Cut through the paper to score line. Fold the edges inward along score lines. Glue the edges together. Bring ends together to form a circle. Glue.

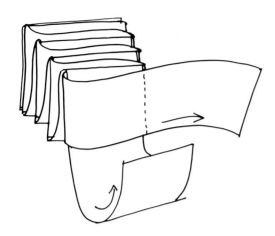

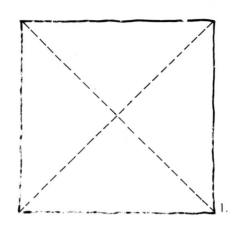

Making a ribbon garland:
Cut 2 pieces of ribbon to desired length. Overlap as shown at right, and staple together. Fold one ribbon over the other, repeating until the length of ribbon is used. Staple ends together.

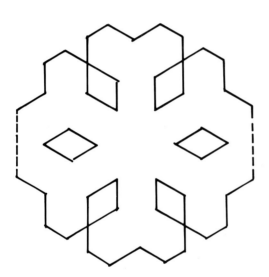

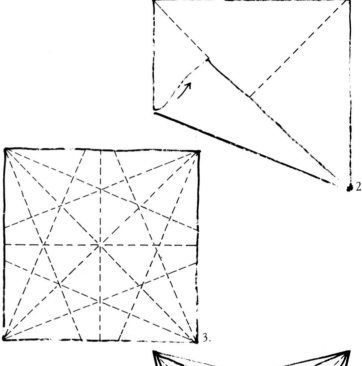

Making a snowflake ribbon:
Accordion-fold the length of ribbon that's needed. Cut around the edges in the desired snowflake pattern. For the interior design, fold in half diagonally and make small cuts.

Making a gift box:
Use any size square piece of paper. Twice fold in half diagonally as in first diagram. Score folds. Fold one corner in to center crease, as shown in second diagram. Repeat folding on all sides until square resembles third diagram. Gather outer edges and fold inward, following fourth diagram. For an ornament, glue or tape points together at top, as in fifth diagram.

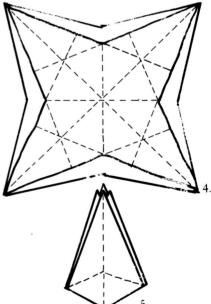

166

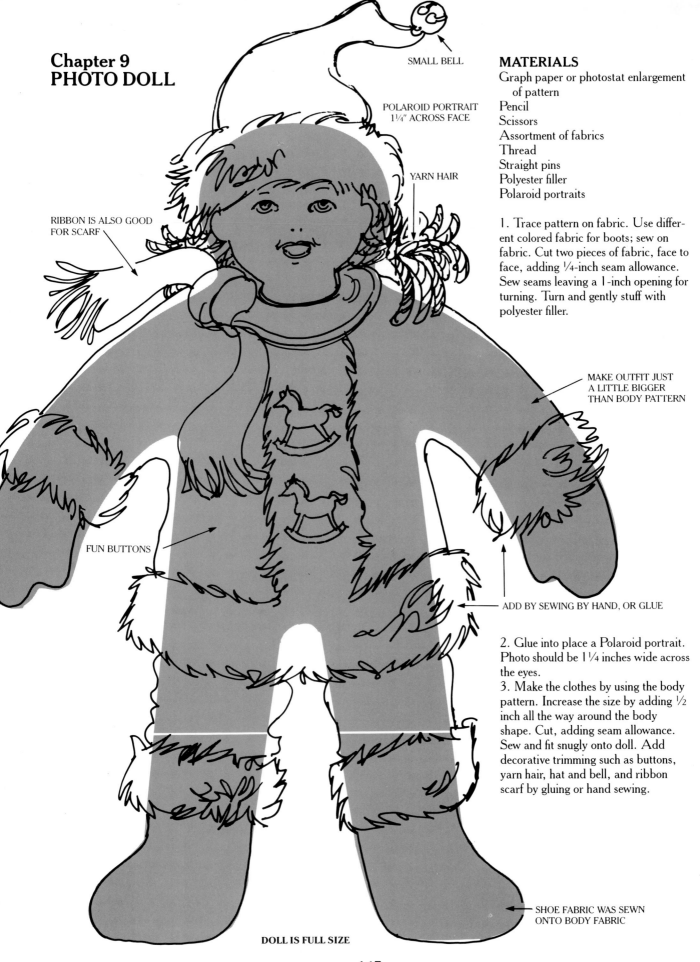

Chapter 9
PHOTO DOLL

SMALL BELL

POLAROID PORTRAIT
1¼" ACROSS FACE

YARN HAIR

RIBBON IS ALSO GOOD
FOR SCARF

MAKE OUTFIT JUST
A LITTLE BIGGER
THAN BODY PATTERN

FUN BUTTONS

ADD BY SEWING BY HAND, OR GLUE

SHOE FABRIC WAS SEWN
ONTO BODY FABRIC

DOLL IS FULL SIZE

MATERIALS
Graph paper or photostat enlargement
    of pattern
Pencil
Scissors
Assortment of fabrics
Thread
Straight pins
Polyester filler
Polaroid portraits

1. Trace pattern on fabric. Use different colored fabric for boots; sew on fabric. Cut two pieces of fabric, face to face, adding ¼-inch seam allowance. Sew seams leaving a 1-inch opening for turning. Turn and gently stuff with polyester filler.

2. Glue into place a Polaroid portrait. Photo should be 1¼ inches wide across the eyes.

3. Make the clothes by using the body pattern. Increase the size by adding ½ inch all the way around the body shape. Cut, adding seam allowance. Sew and fit snugly onto doll. Add decorative trimming such as buttons, yarn hair, hat and bell, and ribbon scarf by gluing or hand sewing.

VISUAL FAMILY PHOTO ARCHIVE

The cutouts, made from either sugar pine or foam core, stand on bases that can be arranged on a mantel, table, or under the Christmas tree, crèche-style. If figures are to be finished on both sides, "flopped" prints must be made for each figure. Otherwise, the heads and tails will not be facing in the right directions.

MATERIALS
For smaller cutouts
Good negatives
Various size prints (some flopped)
3M spray adhesive
Sugar pine or foam core for bases and
    backing
Coping saw or X-Acto knife

For large zebra
Blowups of prints
2 × 4-inch framing
3⁄4-inch plywood panels
Saber saw
Nails and glue
Pull cord, wood bead
Small wood wheels

Editing film for a cutout project
To get a cutout project started, it helps to first have inexpensive proof sheets made of all black and white negatives. If color slides are being used for the blowups, a tabletop light box or photo sorter is an excellent aid.

Once the sharpest negative has been selected, two prints should be ordered or made of each subject, one of them with the image flopped. Then each print is spray-mounted onto an 8-by-10-inch block of sugar pine or a piece of foam core, whichever is preferred.

When the wood-mounted units are dry, the figures are silhouetted with a coping saw. Figures mounted on foam core should be cut with an X-Acto knife. Finally, bases are cut for each image and are glued to form.

Expanding on the idea
Color can be injected into the cutout project either through color prints or hand-painted detailing. Even a color print can be helped with additional, brushed-on shadings.

3⁄4 ✕

168

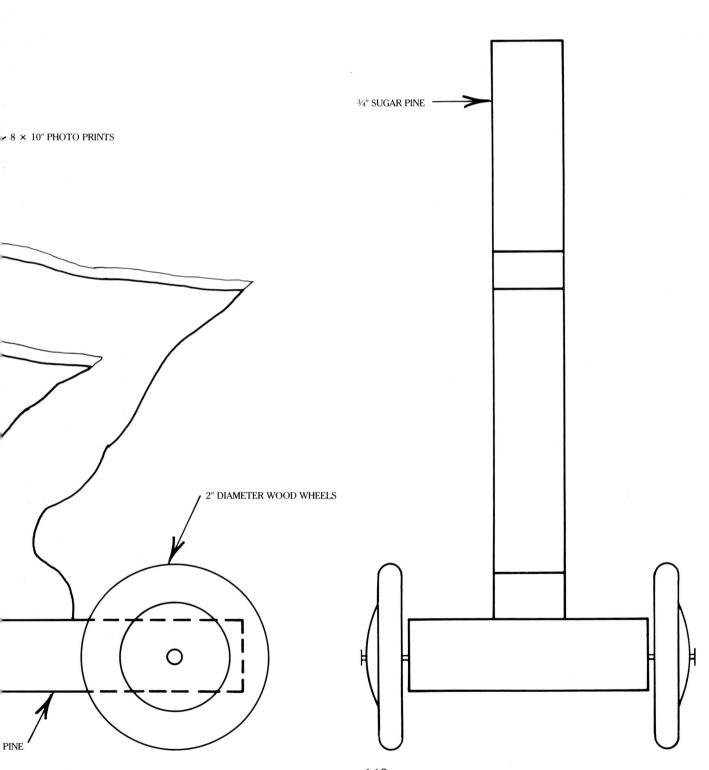

8 × 10″ PHOTO PRINTS

¾″ SUGAR PINE →

2″ DIAMETER WOOD WHEELS

PINE

169

Building the roll-about zebra sculpture

Although a small animal cutout is sturdy, this larger zebra needs a more substantial frame.

The extra measurements should be worked out after the two blowup prints have been made and glued to the ¾-inch plywood mounts. This will ensure a more perfect fit, since not all animal portraits will be exactly like the one used here.

With the mounted silhouette at hand, it's easy to plan the framing. The upright elements should be positioned directly behind legs; the cantilevered support for the head should be designed to suit the particular animal.

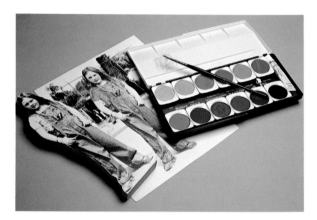

170

For example, an elephant blowup might require additional support in back of its trunk.

The rope tail is a nice surprise; it adds a bit of realism to most animal forms.

An easy way to tow the smaller cutouts
This mini-gaggle of Tulare geese has been temporarily fastened to a sugar pine pull-toy for a fast ride through the backyard. Double-faced masking tape will hold them long enough for most youngsters; nails or glue might be needed for longer runs.

The wooden wheels are stock items found at many builder-supply or lum-ber dealers; the wood bead topping off the pull cord is another easy-to-find accessory.

Be sure to align photographic prints so that the outline is perfect. Small imperfections in the cutting-out process can be duplicated on the opposite side. It's more important to match images on one cutout than to duplicate all finished forms. No two cutouts will ever be exact replicas.

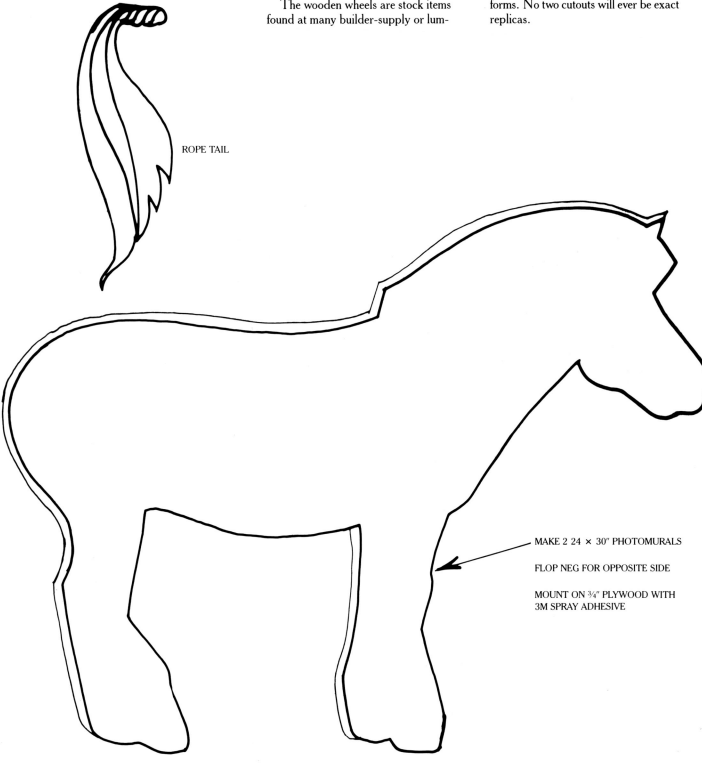

ROPE TAIL

MAKE 2 24 × 30″ PHOTOMURALS

FLOP NEG FOR OPPOSITE SIDE

MOUNT ON ¾″ PLYWOOD WITH 3M SPRAY ADHESIVE

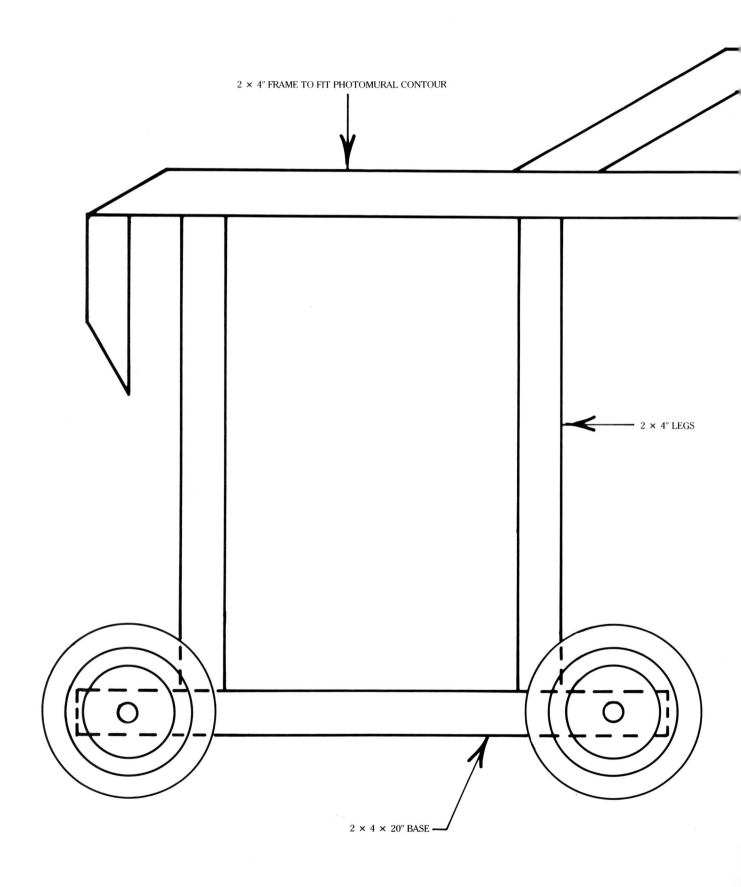

2 × 4″ FRAME TO FIT PHOTOMURAL CONTOUR

2 × 4″ LEGS

2 × 4 × 20″ BASE

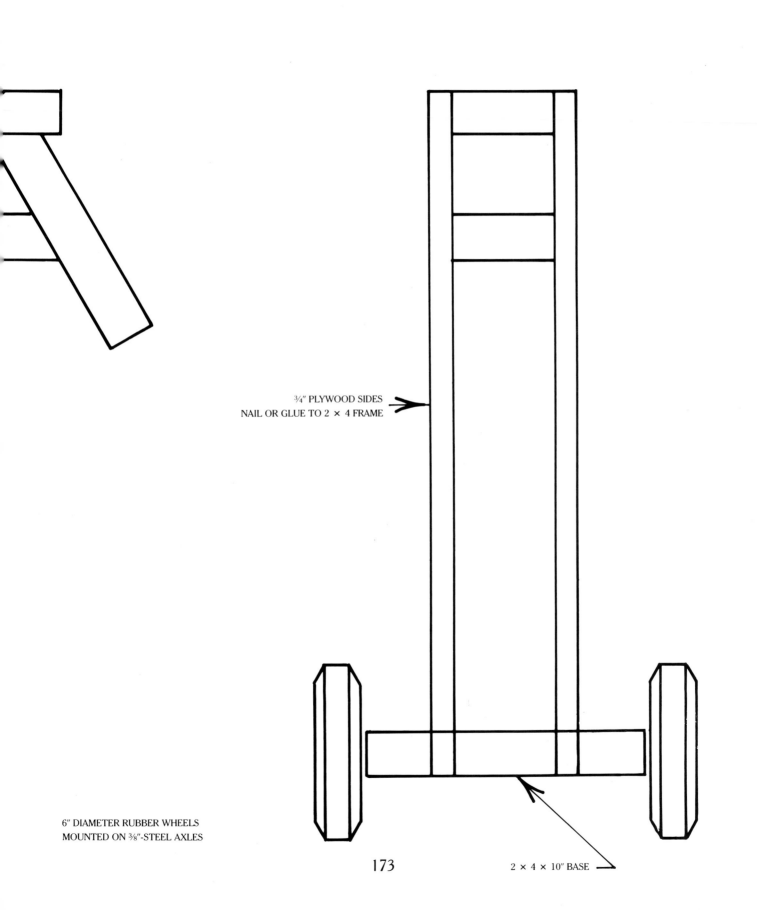

¾" PLYWOOD SIDES
NAIL OR GLUE TO 2 × 4 FRAME

6" DIAMETER RUBBER WHEELS
MOUNTED ON ⅜"-STEEL AXLES

2 × 4 × 10" BASE

Acknowledgments

Although it may appear that this book is filled with my own designs, it is impossible for me to take credit for all of the ideas and hard work that has made this book possible.

To the suppliers whose materials are featured here, many thanks: The Brass Tree, Beverly Hills; H.G. Daniels; Geary's, Beverly Hills; Barbara Goldman, Malibu Art and Design; Helmut Hoffman, Pfaff Sewing Machine; James Ishihara, A and I Lab; Maureen Labro, Savoir Faire; Jeannine Levinthal, Faire La Cuisine; Bill Mackin, Bullock's; Parrish Baking Company; Cal Peterson, Robinson's; Murray Pepper, Home Silk Shop; The Pottery Barn, South Coast Plaza. Thanks, too, are in order to the models in the photographs: Edean Amador, Karin Bellomy, Shawn and Nol Ericson, Tanya Ericson, Richard Hartley, Barbara Hartley, Micole Kalifon, Heather and Dominique Navarro, and Craig Perronne.

Then there are two special people who have contributed greatly. I want to express my warmest thoughts to a most creative lady, Carolyn Murray, my editor at the *Los Angeles Times Home* magazine for ten years. Her ideas led to many of the projects included here. And I would never have finished anything without the talent and tireless energy of my husband and favorite photographer, Max Navarro. As a photojournalist, Max more than captures a moment on film; his brilliant photography has always made my work shine.

This book is an example of creative input from so many other friends, acquaintances, and family. I want to add a special thank you to my other sources of inspiration, my daughters Heather and Dominique.

Dawn Navarro

Photography Credits

The authors and the publisher wish to thank the photographers who contributed to the book:

Hans Albers: *30 (above), 33, 51, 83 (bottom), 95, 98, 99*

Brent Bear: *46, 47, 122, 124*

Richard Clark: *59*

George de Gennaro: *82, 83 (top), 86*

Tom Engler: *74*

Jerry Fruchtman: *54, 55*

Doug Kennedy: *3, 90*

Brian Leatart: *22, 58, 110*

Elyse Lewin: *89*

Max Navarro: *10, 11, 14, 15, 16, 18, 19, 26, 27, 30 (bottom), 31, 32, 34, 35, 38, 39, 40, 41, 42, 43, 44, 45, 50, 55, 62, 63, 64, 66, 67, 69, 70, 71, 72, 73, 76, 78, 79, 91, 94, 102, 103, 106, 107, 108, 109, 114, 115, 117, 118, 119, 120, 127, 128, 134, 138, 139, 147, 154, 158, 159, 170, and jacket photograph*

Patterns, line drawings, and calligraphy by Dawn Navarro

The authors and publisher gratefully acknowledge the generous assistance of Angela Rinaldi at the *Los Angeles Times* Syndicate.

Harry N. Abrams, Inc., offers a selection of wall and engagement calendars. For details on ordering, please write:
Harry N. Abrams, Inc., 100 Fifth Avenue, New York, N.Y. 10011